Beach Handball for Beginners

Springer Nature More Media App

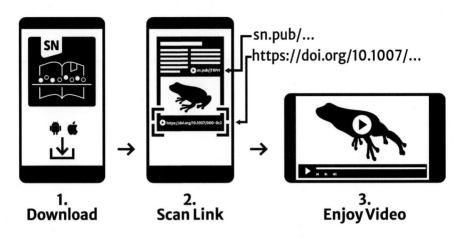

sn.pub/...
https://doi.org/10.1007/...

1.
Download

2.
Scan Link

3.
Enjoy Video

Support: customerservice@springernature.com

Frowin Fasold · Alexander Gehrer · Stefanie Klatt

Beach Handball for Beginners

History, Organization, Rules and Gameplay

 Springer

Frowin Fasold
Institute of Exercise Training
and Sport Informatics,
Department Cognitive and Team,
Racket Sport Research
German Sport University Cologne
Köln, Nordrhein-Westfalen, Germany

Alexander Gehrer
Göppingen, Germany

Stefanie Klatt
Institute of Exercise Training
and Sport Informatics,
Department Cognitive and Team,
Racket Sport Research
German Sport University Cologne
Köln, Nordrhein-Westfalen, Germany

ISBN 978-3-662-64565-9   ISBN 978-3-662-64566-6   (eBook)
https://doi.org/10.1007/978-3-662-64566-6

This work contains media enhancements, which are displayed with a "play" icon. Material in the print book can be viewed on a mobile device by downloading the Springer Nature "More Media" app available in the major app stores. The media enhancements in the online version of the work can be accessed directly by authorized users.

Coverfoto © F. Fasold, A. Gehrer, S. Klatt

This Springer Spektrum imprint is published by the registered company Springer-Verlag GmbH, DE part of Springer Nature.
The registered company address is: Heidelberger Platz 3, 14197 Berlin, Germany

Foreword

On behalf of the European handball community, we wholeheartedly welcome another quality book on the sport, and especially a document that focuses on the branch of beach handball. Alex Gehrer has been a part of the EHF family for more than 20 years, and within our family, he has filled many roles; he qualified as a beach handball referee and delegate, then continued through the realm of the sport by becoming a lecturer, often presenting on the EHF Competence Academy & Network (CAN) circuit. When Gehrer joined EHF Marketing GmbH in 2010, the marketing arm of the European Handball Federation, he took on leading business development tasks overseeing bidding processes for club team final events such as the inaugural EHF Cup Final Tournament, as well as principally assuming the responsibility for project and concept management, particularly for the Women's EHF Champions League.

This body of work is a natural development for the former German national beach handball team coach. Alex Gehrer is a true expert in his field, and the collaboration with the Deutsche Sporthochschule Köln (German Sport University Cologne), specifically with Prof. Dr. Stefanie Klatt and Dr. Frowin Fasold, provides a clear indication to the significance and proficiency that this book presents. The European Handball Federation began its cooperation with the German Sport University Cologne in February 2014 when we successfully launched the 'European Handball Manager' certification programme. Currently in its seventh year, the partnership of the EHF with this renowned institute continues to have a crucial role in the development of the sport at the executive level. Thus, the veracity of the information contained in *Beach Handball for Beginners* is given.

Now, this axis of expertise invites the reader, whether a novice or a veteran, to take a journey into the rousing domain of beach handball, presenting the discipline as the first offshoot from the indoor version of the sport that is exhibited and organised on the beaches across Europe. From its origins, the book gives a comprehensive overview of the origins of the sport and its spirit, underlining the value of its motto 'Fair Play'; it also shows the longevity and inclusivity of the activity as it engages both youth and senior players. The adaptability of beach handball is seen in the chapter that focuses on the development of skills as the game of handball is introduced to beginners entering the game, and activates implicit learning processes through play, but keeps the game at the heart of sporting education.

The authors have created an encyclopaedic guide that will serve as an indispensable component for the reader wanting to become more familiar with beach handball. In this well-rounded publication, they do not miss a step as they cover tactical and technical elements of beach handball, providing guidelines for the area of methods and training, in addition to a thorough exploration into the field of officiating, and this script furthermore introduces the reader to beach handball event organisation.

It will come as no surprise when, years down the line, this beach handball codex becomes recommended reading chosen by educators when implementing beach handball instruction. For now, we wish you an enjoyable read and look forward to seeing you on the beach!

EHF President Michael Wiederer (Photo: EHF)

European Handball Federation   Michael Wiederer
Vienna, Austria June 2021

Preface

Sports, especially team sports, have always had a dynamic character. Sometimes a game develops in a gradual, step-by-step manner, and sometimes it is just unpredictable and volatile. Handball is a perfect example of this ever-changing character. In the past two years, a sub-discipline within handball—beach handball—which first came into prominence in the 1990s, has become increasingly important. We, the authors of this book, recognize the growing significance of beach handball and, therefore, have focused on it in this book.

We see a high potential in beach handball to foster participation and enthusiasm for beginners and children in playing as a team. It is an enjoyable game to pick up and has the power to sustain long-lasting support and interest. Beach handball should not be seen as only a handball discipline played by indoor handball players in the summer. It extends well beyond that by presenting the overall values and the philosophy of the game of handball in an outdoor setting and while supporting team spirit. The aim of this book, therefore, is to show people that irrespective of their motor abilities and skills in handball, beach handball is a fun and exciting sport that is easy to take on and sustain for a long time.

The contents of the book discuss recent concepts in the development of the sport, the pedagogical, psychological, and sociological aspects, and the exercise and movement sciences involved in picking up beach handball. The three of us have been significantly involved personally in the beach handball community, and we have developed this work based on our experiences. Alexander Gehrer was one of the pioneers of this game in Germany. Frowin Fasold has been instrumental in developing the game further and is now the female youth national coach in Germany. Stefanie Klatt is a professional beach volleyball player and an accomplished sports scientist, bringing with her the expertise of playing a sand-based sport. All of us have found a great deal of interest in beach handball and the way it has developed in the past few decades. Based on our collective experience and knowledge, we have developed this work as a landmark text in this discipline.

We thank the entire beach handball community in Europe wholeheartedly because without their great support, openness, and critical feedback, this work would not be possible. A big thank-you goes to Merle Ninse and Deborah Seipp, who were instrumental in shortlisting the contents of this book. We also thank, in particular, the European Handball Federation for their consistent support.

Beach Handball for Beginners is a fundamental work that could be used to promote beach handball in a variety of contexts (e.g., school, clubs, federations, sports communities), independent of the level of ability of the players. We encourage all our readers an enjoyable foray into the exciting world of beach handball, with the main characteristics of the game in mind: respect, fair play, action, and enjoyment.

Köln, Germany   Frowin Fasold
Göppingen, Germany   Alexander Gehrer
Köln, Germany   Stefanie Klatt

Contents

Introduction

The following chapter provides an introduction and an overview of the contents of the book.

Play has always been a basic human need and can be found in many different forms of social interaction. Sports represent a special form of play that can captivate many people around the world. Toward the end of the twentieth century, the discipline of beach handball developed from the sport of handball and has been attracting more and more people worldwide. This discipline combines elements from indoor handball with free, creative game actions and the positive effects of the sun, the beach, and the joy of playing (see Fig. 1.1).

The first part of this book is intended to give people who are not familiar with handball the opportunity to know the history and the fair play concept of beach handball. It indicates the advantages that beach handball offers for beginners in handball as well as children who wish to start playing handball.

The next section of the book provides basic information on the set of rules for players at the beginner level and discusses a holistic approach to teaching. Through this approach, training can be given for the various phases of a beach handball game simultaneously. This training is supplemented with tips on coaching behaviour and on the organization and methodological-didactic design of training or teaching sessions. Finally, for basic understanding, an overview of the playing positions and game functions, as well as attack and defence formations common in beach handball, is presented.

The core of the book is the following chapter on developing skills and abilities for implementing play with beginners. The game forms presented are intended to activate implicit learning processes through play and to keep play at the centre of the learning process in each learning step. The presented sequence of learning steps

Fig. 1.1 Free and dynamic play in beach handball (Photo: EHF)

is not binding and can be adapted and extended at any time. It should develop in a flexible manner and promote the ability to play.

The next chapter of the book takes an in-depth look at basic tactical and technical elements of beach handball.

For training in individual technical-tactical elements, which are especially important for beginners, content and methodological suggestions are made in the next section of the book. The training of cooperative and collective game elements is also discussed here. Helpful tips are given on the training of athletes. The chapter concludes with in-depth information on coaching in competition and game analysis in beach handball.

Because referees and officials not only are critical to the implementation of competitions, but are also seen as instrumental in the general development of the game, this aspect is addressed in the penultimate chapter. This part is followed by information on the organization of a beach handball tournament and the construction of beach handball fields. The chapter concludes with references to existing textbooks, literature, and materials in various languages, which also discuss beach handball at the beginner level.

The contents of the book are based on the authors' experiences and opinions, which have evolved over time. Extensive experience, not only in beach handball but also in other sports, and detailed evaluations should make the contents as functional and easy to implement as possible. To add further value to the contents of this book, existing knowledge has been utilized as well. However, to enhance the readability, scientific citations are not used throughout the book (except in literal quotations). Throughout the book, no distinction is made in terminology between student, athlete, or participant. The authors use the term athlete, which refers to all the people involved in a game or training. Although the term athlete is often associated with a trained athlete in competitive sports, for the authors all the people who play or train in beach handball are athletes, independent of age, gender, or performance level.

Origin, Philosophy, and Advantages of Beach Handball

2

Contents

Beach Handball and Indoor Handball: One Sport, Two Disciplines

In the following chapter, a general historical background shows that several game disciplines have been united under the label of the sport handball since its inception. Although the history of beach handball is discussed later in the book, the current role of the two disciplines, indoor and beach handball, is

(continued)

Supplementary Information The online version contains supplementary material available at [https://doi.org/10.1007/978-3-662-64566-6_2]. The videos can be accessed by scanning the related images with the SN More Media App.

5

shown, and differentiations in their nature from other alternative forms of handball are highlighted. There are also detailed accounts of how both disciplines benefit from each other.

From the historical perspective, the birth of the handball sport can be seen during the transition from the nineteenth to the twentieth century. In various European countries, there have been developments in game forms that can be seen as the basis for indoor handball as it is known today. However, this form of indoor handball developed primarily based on the field handball game, which was played in the open air on a large field (soccer field) with 11 players in each team. At the beginning of the twentieth century, traditional handball played in large fields was set to become the number one national sport in some countries. The handball finals in the 1936 Olympic Games in Berlin took place in front of more than 100,000 spectators. The sport of handball seemed to spread rapidly in the world.

Despite its initial success, field handball could not establish itself in the long term among competitive sports and was finally replaced by indoor handball in the middle of the twentieth century. The reasons for the failure of field handball are primarily in the rules (the playing field was too large; there was little space for action because of a three-part division of the playing field into zones, creating a vacuum in the midfield leading to inactivity of some players; the ball was too large, etc.) and the permanent superiority of the German teams (the German field handball national team, for example, won the 1938 World Cup final against Switzerland 23–0). Attempts to change the rules, such as changing the ball size from 68 to 71 cm to 60 to 64 cm, the introduction of the double catch, the offside rule, and much more, contributed to the lack of transparency of the game for spectators.

In the middle of the twentieth century, indoor handball became more and more popular. The higher international equality of opportunity in indoor handball compared to full-field handball was certainly a decisive factor in its rapid development. Furthermore, the faster and more dynamic indoor handball was seen as more likely to meet the expectations of the players and spectators after a competitive game than the relatively undynamic field handball, which was characterized by spaces without action. The evolution of modern handball probably began with the inclusion of indoor handball in the Olympic schedule in Munich in 1972. With establishment on the small field, in addition to numerous tactical skills, the technique and condition of the players improved. In the opinion of many experts, indoor handball had developed into a "...hard, sometimes brutal fighting game." (Weichert 1978, p. 23) at the end of the 1970s. In the 1980 Olympic final in Moscow between the German Democratic Republic (GDR) and the Republics of the Soviet Union (UdSSR), 424 fouls were recorded on video. The handball game threatened to drift into an overtly hard and brutal fighting game, which was no longer accepted as a sporting competition, not in the least by the spectators.

The new version of the indoor handball rules of August 1, 1981, by the International Handball Federation (IHF)—in particular, Rule 8 (behaviour towards opponents) and Rule 17 (punishments)—succeeded in curbing the harshness and brutality in handball. It was also successful in maintaining the open competitive character of the handball game for players and spectators. Further rule changes (fast-throw-on, possible time-out of 1 min per half, mandatory "time out" in various situations, passive warning signs, etc.) allowed more offensive and anticipatory defensive formations and more creative attacking play to be identified in the period that followed. All these effects not only seemed to maintain the competitive character of indoor handball, but also gave it a new dimension. Beach handball first appeared at the end of the twentieth century.

From the beginning of the implementation of handball games, several disciplines are united under the sport of handball. The history of the beach handball discipline is examined in detail again in the next chapter.

Although the discipline of field handball is no longer played in competitions, indoor handball is currently the most successful discipline in the sport of handball in terms of sporting and economic development. The discipline of beach handball, however, has been attracting more and more people with increasing professionalism and has long since made it out of the mass sport category. When considering the various disciplines of handball, wheelchair handball, which has been gaining more and more attention worldwide in recent years, especially in conversations around inclusive sports, should not be ignored.

In addition to these handball disciplines, which are characterized by competition structures, official regulations, and competitive sports orientations, there are a large number of alternative handball variants. Forms of play such as Goalcha™, five-a-side handball, 4 + 1 mini handball, handball on grass, snow handball, or ultimate handball are freer in their designs and interpretations and usually only follow recommended rules and no fixed framework and international competition structures.

After this distinction between handball disciplines and alternative handball variants, the disciplines of beach and indoor handball should be brought into discourse once again (see Fig. 2.1).

It is not unusual for a sport to differentiate itself into two or more disciplines down to the level of an Olympic sport. Volleyball is practiced at the highest level, both indoors and outdoors in the sand. In basketball, the 3×3 discipline has developed next to the traditional 5-on-5 discipline. Although hockey is an Olympic

Fig. 2.1 Different conditions, different disciplines, but one sport

discipline on the field, indoor hockey does not have the same standing, but it is also practiced internationally on a competitive sports level.

The development of a sport in several disciplines is, however, still viewed critically in handball, with the beach and indoor variants currently seen as problematic. The concern that the discipline of beach handball will compete with the discipline of indoor handball can and must be regarded as void. Most beach handball players are also active as indoor handball players; very few migrate to the sand discipline. In Europe, this is currently mostly because beach handball only follows a structured competition plan in the summer months, when indoor handball is inactive. Beach handball also offers the opportunity for athletes to remain engaged with the sport after their indoor career has ended. Beach handball offers nations that do not have the infrastructure for professional indoor handball operations the opportunity to find members and arouse enthusiasm for the game.

Handball halls may not be always easy to play in, especially during the summer months in countries with higher temperatures, and especially for children and young people with no experience of handball, but the beach handball discipline does not have this limitation. Beach handball can, therefore, also serve as a supplier for indoors handball. If the enthusiasm for handball in the sand is sustained, the joy of playing indoors will not diminish.

Beach handball discipline benefits from the skills and abilities that are acquired in indoor handball, and indoor handball can also benefit from the skills and abilities required in the beach handball discipline. In addition to the increasingly necessary anticipatory and active game behaviour because of the constant over- and outnumbered game along with the limited possibilities of bouncing the ball, playing on sand can also have a preventive character, which has a positive effect on the performance of an athlete in indoors handball. In indoor handball there can be a "Crunch Time" situation at the end of a game, but this pressure situation can arise up to five times per game in beach handball (see Fig. 2.2). Every set has to be decided, possibly in "golden goal" situations. The shoot-out that represents a pressure situation, and which in indoor handball is comparable to a 7-m throw, occurs only extremely rarely in beach handball. Dealing with such pressure situations can, therefore, be especially trained for and encouraged in indoor handball; the transfer of skills to indoor handball is, thus, extremely likely because of the proximity of the two disciplines.

> In conclusion, beach handball and indoor handball should be seen as two disciplines of a sport, not as competitors. Rather, the two disciplines support each other and can only benefit from each other as parts of the sport of handball.

Fig. 2.2 Success and failing in one picture (Photo: EHF)

The History of Beach Handball

The following chapter describes the historical development of the handball discipline beach handball. Here, international developments and exemplary regional developments are the focus. The level of performance in beach handball and a qualitative and quantitative analysis are also discussed. Structural aspects of the game concerning competition formats and its integration into professional associations are also examined.

Origin and Spread

The short history of the sport of beach handball can be traced back to 1990. The chairman of the promotions department of the Italian National Olympic Committee (CONI), Professor Briani, came up with the idea of taking other sports to the beach, based on the successes of beach volleyball in the 1990s.

Professor Bartolini, who was responsible for school handball at the Italian National Handball Federation (FIGH) at the time, took up the task and put together the first set of rules for the new game. To use existing beach volleyball courts, the playing field and the number of players were reduced compared to indoor handball.

To make the game faster and more attractive, the entire sidelines were defined as a substitution area.

The entire concept disappeared into oblivion for two years. Then, in 1992, on the *Isola di Ponza*, a small island in southern Italy, Gianni Buttarelli (then president of the Sequax Lazio handball team) and Franco Schiano (then president of Serie B Handball Teams in Italy) took up the idea of *Beach Handball*. Two international referees (indoor handball) from Italy, Di Piero and Masi, were asked to lead the games and to evaluate the rules together with Professor Bartolini.

Based on the experience of these games, initial work was carried out on the attractiveness of the sport of *Beach Handball*: "Balls caught and thrown in the air" (nowadays called "inflight" in beach handball, "alley-oop" in basketball, or "Kempa trick" in indoor handball) as well as goals by the goalkeeper were rewarded with an extra point and header goals with two extra points. The method of counting with two separately rated sets and a shoot-out (defined as "one against the goalkeeper" at the time) had already been introduced. Everything was designed to make the game as spectacular as possible for participants and spectators.

In the same year, Buttarelli and Schiano founded the Comitato Organizzatore Handball Beach (COHB) in Italy, which is the world's first organized association for beach handball. Under the leadership of the COHB, the first official international beach handball tournament series with four demonstration tournaments took place in the Italian region of Lazio in the summer of 1993 (see Fig. 2.3). In addition to some Italian teams, participants included a junior selection from Algeria, the Russian team Poliot, a military selection from Italy, and a junior selection from TSV Bartenbach

Fig. 2.3 First official international beach handball tournament series in 1993 in Lazio (Photo: Alex Gehrer)

(Germany). Media and television reported on this tournament series, and thus helped to convey the image of the new sport *Beach Handball*.

With these developments, international interest in beach handball also grew steadily. As early as 1993, representatives of the Dutch Handball Federation (NHV) engaged with the rules for this new game. In May 1994, Beach Handball was officially recognized by the International Handball Federation (IHF).

In September 1994, the first internationally endorsed rules for beach handball were laid down at the IHF Congress in Harleem (Netherlands). In addition to a demonstration game (Italy against the Netherlands), the first videotapes about beach handball were also given out to the attending congress participants at this congress by the COHB. This congress led to a rapid spread of beach handball worldwide.

Although the COHB was finally dissolved, the game established itself in Italy, and a beach handball tour was held there on various beaches, with the final in Naples, as early as 1994. In the years that followed, the tour grew steadily. Italy was also able to play a pioneering role in the first international comparisons in beach handball. In particular, the Italian women's selection established itself among the world's best in beach handball.

Brazil hosted the world's first national team tournament in Rio de Janeiro in January 1995, using the rules proposed by the COHB. The national teams from Brazil, Portugal, Argentina, and Italy fought for the first title, which the hosts eventually secured. In the same year, the EHF also set up a special working group consisting of Jesus Guerrero from Spain, Ton van Linder from the Netherlands, Ralf Dejaco from Italy, and Helmut Hoeritsch from Austria in the EHF Methodology Commission to evaluate the beach handball rules.

National Development (Example of Germany)

The following section illustrates the national development of the sport of beach handball in Germany as an example. In many other countries in Europe and worldwide, there were similar developments and controversies, which are discussed later.

The joy of this attractive game allowed the TSV Bartenbach junior team to develop the idea of importing this novel game, which they learnt in Italy in 1993, to Germany. With adequate support from the German Handball Federation (DHB), the Handball Association Württemberg (HVW) as well as the media and sponsors, the first beach handball facility in Germany was completed for World Handball Day on June 23, 1994 (see Fig. 2.4). For the inauguration of the facility, the beach pioneers from Bartenbach competed against a DHB selection.

The reactions to the first beach handball tournament in Germany were consistently positive. Participants, spectators, and handball experts present at the event were enthusiastic. The then indoor handball national trainer of the DHB, Arno Ehret, put it in a nutshell: "Handball needs attractive fun offers. The event in Bartenbach impressively demonstrated what can be achieved with beach handball." (Ehret in Steinle 1994, p. 36).

Fig. 2.4 First beach handball tournament in Germany in 1994 in Bartenbach (Photo: Alex Gehrer)

Since then, more than 50 beach handball tournaments in all performance and age classes have been held in Bartenbach. In the years that followed, more than 30 beach handball facilities were built in the Baden-Württemberg region, and the initial scepticism quickly turned into pure enthusiasm for the new game.

In 1995 the DHB started a test project with five beach handball tournaments (in Bartenbach, Warnemünde, St. Peter-Ording, Darß, and Westerland) as a test run for a tournament series. In the following year, the first DHB Beach Handball Masters series with 15 preliminary tournaments and a grand final was held in Westerland (Sylt). More than 10,000 spectators followed the games on the beach on the five playing fields with great interest.

In the following years, the enthusiasm for beach handball grew steadily in Germany. Cuxhaven on the North Sea had established itself as the "Mecca of the German beach handball scene" and the venue for all final tournaments. From 1999 to 2007 the official German Beach Handball Championships were held here with great success by the DHB. In 2006, Germany even hosted the Beach Handball European Championships for men and women in Cuxhaven.

However, in 2007 the executive committee of the DHB suddenly decided not to further promote beach handball and all efforts in this direction were ended. In 2015, the DHB overturned the presidium's decision from 2007 and, for the first time, held the German beach handball championships, which were carried out in 2015 at a relatively small facility in Kassel as a test project. Since 2016, the German Beach

Handball Championships have been taking place in a more prominent setting on the Berlin Mitte beach area and are generating growing enthusiasm among teams, spectators, and sponsors. In 2020, the German Beach Handball Championships was finally scheduled to return to Cuxhaven on the North Sea, but this was postponed by the COVID pandemic. The DHB has also been participating in international competitions with beach handball national teams since 2015.

International Development

In the mid-1990s, beach handball had developed very differently in individual countries. There were already organized series of tournaments in Italy, Spain, and Germany. In the other Mediterranean countries as well as in Scandinavia, individual tournaments were organized on the beaches. In the countries without access to a sea, numerous beach handball facilities were built on the club's own sports fields. Beach handball in France developed its own: under the name "sandball", the French mainly focused on fun, disembodied games, and spectacular actions; the result was secondary.

In addition to many national efforts, since the turn of the millennium it has primarily been the international associations that have given the young sport of beach handball a new profile through national team competitions.

European Championships

In July 2000, the European Handball Federation (EHF) held the first European Beach Handball Championships. On the beach of Gaeta (near Rome, Italy), the first international contests were held for a week. Eight teams each in the male and female categories of the tournament competed for the first international title.

In addition to the countries bordering the Mediterranean, participants were mainly Eastern European countries and the Netherlands for women. Germany also took part in the tournament with two teams (one male and one female). The winner of this tournament was to qualify directly for the Beach Handball World Championship in Rio de Janeiro (Brazil) in February 2001. Belarus was the first European champion in the men's league (against Spain in the final), whereas Ukraine prevailed against Germany in the women's league. It turned out that in international beach handball at that time, an outstanding goalkeeper and a powerful playmaker (specialist) were the keys to success. The Eastern European teams were able to assert themselves with strength and athleticism against the more experimental and playful Mediterranean countries as well as Germany and the Netherlands.

Since then, European beach handball championships have been held every two years with a steadily growing number of participants (since 2007, in odd years, so as not to clash with the world championships introduced in 2004).

World Games

The World Games unite those sports that are not part of the program of the Olympic Games but are nonetheless widespread worldwide and/or are interested in one day being included in the canon of the Olympic Games. They are held every four years in different locations, in the year after the Summer Olympics. The host is the "International World Games Association" (IWGA) under the patronage of the International Olympic Committee (IOC).

The World Championships in Rio de Janeiro (Brazil) scheduled for February 2001 were cancelled at short notice. As a replacement, the 2001 World Games in Akita (Japan) were upgraded to the status of unofficial world championships. The results of the finals at the 2001 World Games in Akita were identical to those of the 2000 European Championships in Gaeta: Belarus won the men's competition beating Spain, and Ukraine won the women's competition, beating the German team.

At the World Games in Akita (Japan) in 2001 and Duisburg (Germany) in 2005, beach handball was still a demonstration sport. Beach handball has been an integral part of the World Games since 2009 in Kaohsiung (Taiwan) and an absolute magnet for spectators for the games (10,000 spectators in the final of the Word Games in Cali, Colombia).

World Championships

Since 2004, world championships in beach handball have been held every two years with growing interest. In November 2004 the first official world championships in beach handball took place in El Gouna (Egypt). However, the oceanic and North American launch sites fell into disrepair. Only Brazil from South America participated. Spain and Germany waived their starting place so that Ukraine and Hungary moved up from Europe for men and Hungary also took the starting place for women.

These second intercontinental championships also showed a very clear picture. For women, the Europeans took the first five places, ahead of Brazil, Japan, and Hong Kong. In the men's field, Egypt was the world champion in its own country, beating out the five European countries; Bahrain, Oman, and Brazil were left trailing behind in the overall tally. This picture changed in the years to come. Since the 2006 World Cup in its own country, Brazil has proceeded to become an absolute super power in beach handball (for women and men).

Olympic Games

In 2018 beach handball replaced indoor handball at the Youth Olympic Games in Buenos Aires (Argentina). Beach handball was an absolute crowd-puller at this event and delighted the masses. Beach handball has developed as an independent sport or discipline within a few years. After the continental and world championships, the World Games, and the premiere at the 2018 Youth Olympic Games, it now remains to be seen whether beach handball will also be included in the canon of Olympic sports among seniors soon. Numerous efforts to this end are currently underway.

Performance Level of the Beach Handball Discipline

Qualitative Analysis

Beach handball has developed rapidly from the first European championship in Gaeta (Italy) in 2000 until today. In the beginning, "indoor handball on sand" was mainly played with an outstanding thrower (specialist), but especially in the early years there were many creative accents on the part of the coaches and teams. As anchored in the IHF rules, nowadays, in addition to goals from specialists (formerly the goalkeeper) and 6 m goals, "creative and spectacular goals" (see IHF 2021, rule 9:2) are also rated with an additional point.

Initially, the only creative element that was played was the inflight, in which the ball is thrown to a teammate in the air, and he/she catches it while jumping and throws it at the goal. The inflight is a complex interplay of at least two players in which timing, passing, catching in the air, and finally, the throw from a relatively difficult situation, lead to a fascinating spectacle.

The introduction of the inflight meant that many defensive lines were now located a bit more defensively to prevent a pass. So, a solution had to be found for a two-point rating for a single player. At the 2004 European Championships in Antalya (Turkey), there were many different approaches to solving this problem, for example, some teams made a roll forward or a wheel in front of the goal throw.

At this point, the referees were overwhelmed with the "open rules" and rewarded any "creative or spectacular" approach with two points, and beach handball came under the threat of degenerating into a circus event. To avoid this, clear definitions for "creative and spectacular hits" had to be derived, which provided clear guidelines for all those involved, but unfortunately also limited the creativity of the coaches and players.

As the only other "creative or spectacular element" besides the inflight, the throw from a pirouette movement ("spin shot") has emerged as a remarkable athletic feat (see Fig. 2.5). In this manoeuvre, the player turns 360 degrees in the air, rotates around his/her longitudinal axis before the throw. Nowadays this shot takes up a large part of the individual tactics in beach handball and is shown in different variations (for example, in combination with the inflight or as a double turn).

Quantitative Analysis

A comprehensive scouting and analysis system was introduced for the first time at the Beach Handball World Championships in Cadiz (Spain) in 2008 (see Gehrer and König 2008). It was found that about 20% of all successful throws in the male league and only about 10% in the female league are inflights. Around 40% of the hits are "spin shots" and a little over 20% specialist hits. The women use the tactical element of the one-point hit significantly more often.

In addition to the gender-specific differences, there is also a differentiation concerning the placement of the teams. The top teams use the tactical elements of spin shot and inflight significantly more often than the teams in the lower end of the final tally. These fundamental differences have hardly changed in recent years. The general level of beach handball at the world level seems to have increased slightly

Fig. 2.5 Spin shot at the Junior Beach Handball European Championships 2021 in Varna, Bulgaria (Photo: EHF)

over the years. In the male tournaments, almost 45% of all successful throws are now completed with spin shots and 25% with inflights; among women, it is even more with 50% spin shots and 15% infights (cf. Tezcan 2018).

Another indication of the increase in the international level of beach handball is the number of goals and points per game. In 2004, almost 46 points (women) and 54 points (men) were scored at the first beach handball World Cup in El Gouna (Egypt). With a gradual increase, the values in 2018 were 57 points (women) and 65 points (men).

There is no clear development trends in the game that are decided in the shoot-out; the statistics indicate a wide range between 25 and 60% (per event) at all previous world and European championships. In terms of age or gender, there does not seem to be a clear picture here either. The statistics for successful goalkeepers seem to be relatively stable in beach handball; in the top range, it is between 30 and 35% saved balls. Interestingly, this number is almost identical to the number for goalkeepers in indoor handball, which again speaks for the closeness of the two disciplines to one another (see Fig. 2.6).

There are no major outliers in the morphological data either. The average male beach handball player at a World or European championship is on average between 185 and 195 cm tall and weighs around 90 kg; their female counterpart measures around 175 cm and weighs an average of 70 kg (cf. Tezcan 2018; Zapardiel 2018). A position-specific differentiation has not yet been investigated.

Fig. 2.6 The goalkeeper in beach handball (Photo: EHF)

EHF image video; Standbild Video 01. (▶ https://doi.org/10.1007/000-6c0)

Organizational Structure in Beach Handball

To understand the worldwide organizational structure of beach handball, it is helpful to understand the interaction of the International Olympic Committee (IOC) with the National Olympic Committees (NOC) and the elite sports federations (NF).

The IOC is the highest and the only decisive body for the Olympic Games. Its tasks include processing and regulating all the questions relating to the games. The IOC recognizes the various NOCs, awards the Olympic Games, organizes the Olympic Congress, and sets rules for the Olympic Charter. The NFs are international nongovernmental organizations recognized by the IOC. It is their responsibility to oversee the practice of the sport; they set the rules and technical requirements as well as competition standards nationally. Sports recognized by the IOC as Olympic sports are part of the Olympic Games. This recognition does not necessarily guarantee the inclusion of the sport in the competition program of the Olympic Games (IOC homepage/www.olympic.org).

The IOC also recognizes the NOCs in the sense of acceptance into the Olympic movement. In contrast to the NFs, however, NOCs do not exist independently from the IOC; they derive their justification from the existence of the Olympic movement. The NOCs are run as corporations at the state and country level. In close cooperation with the IOC, the NOCs promote the Olympic movement and send their Olympic teams (IOC homepage, www.olympic.org).

National umbrella organizations (such as the national handball associations, professional associations for Olympic and non-Olympic sports) are affiliated to the NOCs. The athletes of the Olympic sports (winter and summer) alternately coordinate their training control every four years to the absolute highlight "Olympic Games." Top athletes in non-Olympic sports have the goal of participating in the "World Games", which also take place every four years (Homepage Deutscher Olympischer Sportbund, www.dosb.de).

In 2007, the IHF founded the Beach Handball Working Group, which has since managed all beach handball-related themes at the international level (including rule development, organization of world championships, beach handball tournaments at the World Games, and the Youth Olympic Games). Members of this working group are Chairman Giampiero Masi (ITA), Alexander Gehrer (GER), Fernando Posada (ESP), Panos Antoniou (CYP), George Bebetsos (GRE), and Michel Pape (IHF Office).

Beach handball commissions in the continental and national associations were founded in the following years (for example, the EHF Beach Handball Commission in 2008) to handle various issues related to the sport. In addition to the further development of the sport, beach handball commissions in the continental associations mainly focus on the organization of continental championships (at both national and club levels). An example of this is the European Beach Tour (EBT) for club teams of the European Handball Federation (EHF). In addition to conducting national beach handball championships, the national beach handball commissions are primarily concerned with the organization of national teams. At this level (and especially at the regional level) there are topics such as talent scouting,

Fig. 2.7 Regional base training in Bartenbach, Germany (Photo: Alex Gehrer)

talent promotion, training management, and training of referees and coaches (see Fig. 2.7).

In summary, one can say that the sport of beach handball is now integrated into a global organizational structure that is based on the structure of the top sports associations. The rules and frameworks are set by the top committees (IHF Beach Working Group); the foundations for the development of athletes and the sport are largely grounded at a regional level.

Philosophy of Beach Handball

The following chapter considers the game idea and the associated philosophy of the handball discipline, beach handball, as well as its effects on the game itself. The fundamental ideas behind the discipline, namely, fair play, are also discussed. For this purpose, the background, which is determined by the set of rules and the structures, is presented.

The Game Idea

The game idea of a sport describes the goal and course of action of a game. The basic idea of handball is to score goals as a team and to prevent the opposing team from scoring goals by recapturing the ball. This idea can be found in almost all handball disciplines and also in all alternative forms of handball. The respective sets of rules then form the respective discipline or game form. Beach handball, however, differs here. The game idea includes not only throwing, but also scoring points through successful goals. The idea in defensive game actions is to prevent the opposing team from scoring and the opponent from scoring more points than one's own team. The best way to do this is to win the ball, so the opposing team does not score any points. This distinction between "scoring goals" in other handball disciplines and "scoring points" in beach handball seems minimal at first glance. But it has a massive effect on the perception of the game (how is a game played?) and the technical-tactical actions on offense and defence, also based on the rules designed for this purpose.

It is possible to implement the game idea of the other handball disciplines using their specific rules on sand. It should be noted, however, that this will not be considered beach handball, but "handball on sand." In the early years in particular, many beach handball players (players and coaches) who were naturally recruited from indoor handball, predominantly "played handball on sand"; the idea of beach handball as a sport was only implemented over the years by players and coaches.

A game is called beach handball only if the game idea (throwing points, conquering the ball) is implemented according to the beach handball rules and the underlying philosophy. In fact, it does not have to be on sand; beach handball can also be played on other surfaces (hall, lawn, snow), so long as the game idea and the rules are maintained.

Fair Play

The top priority in the beach handball discipline is fair play, which is already included in the preamble of the currently authorized IHF Beach Handball rules (see IHF 2021). This preamble means that all the decisions, in case of doubt, should be made from the point of view of fair play. In particular, the health and integrity of each player should be protected, the spirit and the philosophy of the game should be respected, and the flow of the game should be guaranteed at all times (without, however, tolerating a rule violation or an unauthorized use of advantage).

To ensure and facilitate the attractiveness of the game, both teams should be able to play with full team strength whenever possible. Punishments are, therefore, not punished as team penalties but as individual penalties. Thus, players suspended from the field from irregularities or unsportsmanlike conduct may be replaced or re-enter the field of play only when there has been a change of possession between the two teams. The second suspension of a player causes his/her disqualification (match penalty). Full team strength generally means a 4:3 numerical advantage in beach handball, as the goalkeeper can go into the attack (or can be replaced by a designated specialist) (see Fig. 2.8).

Because of this constantly possible numerical advantage in beach handball, scoring chances are relatively easy to achieve through play. If a goal is scored, the game is restarted directly without a first throw by passing it from the goal area. Free

Fig. 2.8 The 4:3 numerical advantage in beach handball (Photo: Alex Gehrer)

throws are also taken on the spot. Substitutions can be made on practically the entire sidelines of the playing field (minus the goal area). All these conditions lead to the game being played at a very high pace and with a lot of action.

With the quick change from defence to attack and constantly being outnumbered in defence, beach handball practically never creates a solid defence association similar to indoor handball, which requires and makes an almost bodiless game necessary. The defence game does not turn into a physical confrontation but requires skilful coverage of space, constant activity, and the constant use of deception manoeuvres. Fun and exercise through actions, such as diving for the ball in the sand or trying to score a spectacular hit, precede a win at any cost.

Even high deficits in beach handball can be equalized by the additional points and the fact that each half of the game is scored individually: specialist/goalkeeper hits and spectacular hits such as the inflight or the spin shot are scored with an additional point. There is also an additional point when scoring a 6-meter throw. The IHF regulations state: "Both the spirit of the game of Beach Handball and its specific philosophy have to be respected. There has to be space for "creative or spectacular goals," which will be awarded 2 points. A goal is spectacular if it is of high technical standard and it is evidently not a "1-point goal," which is based on fundamental technical skills. A remarkable and dramatic final action may lead to a creative goal. Note: If such goals clearly aim at "ridiculing" the opposing players, it shall

Fig. 2.9 Referee's throw in mini beach handball (Photo: Alex Gehrer)

be considered as unsportsmanlike conduct and shall never lead to a "2-point goal" (Fair Play)" (IHF 2021).

Regarding the fair play concept, the regulation of the additional points emphasises a further specialty. In other handball disciplines, all goals are scored with one point, regardless of how difficult the throw is; in beach handball, an increased level of difficulty (e.g., spin shot) or a special risk (throw by the specialist/goalkeeper leading to an open goal position), as already described, is rewarded with an additional point.

The entire playing time in beach handball consists of two separately rated sets of 10 min each, which are continued in the event of a tie (after the referee's throw) until a team scores the winning goal ("Golden Goal"). The winner of a set receives 1 point. The game begins in each set with a referee's throw (see Fig. 2.9). If one team wins both sets, this team is the overall winner of the game with 2–0 points. If each team wins one set, the winner will be determined by the shoot-out.

Beach handball owes its attractiveness not only to the spectacular throws and the fast counterattack, but also to the shoot-out (see Fig. 2.10). Five players from each team take turns throwing at the opposing goal after the goalkeeper has passed from their goal area, the three-step rule being taken into account, until a final decision has been made. Despite the tension and drama of the shoot-out, the focus here is also on casual contestations, and one tries to outsmart the opposing goalkeeper with a clever trick throw because spectacular hits also count for one extra point in the shoot-out.

This competitive structure of deciding a game over several sets, and not only on the total number of goals/points scored, distinguishes the discipline of beach handball most clearly from all other handball disciplines (indoor handball, field handball, wheelchair handball). This rating system, therefore, also has a special impact on the motivation of the athletes and everyone else involved. Even if a team loses a game,

Fig. 2.10 Shoot-out in beach handball

the chances that they will get at least one point is high. This point not only gives the athletes a positive feeling during the game, but it can also be very important in the further course of a tournament despite the defeat.

In summary, one can say that the sport of beach handball is designed entirely for attractiveness and telegenic; the playing time of 2×10 min (plus possible shoot-out) is calculable, there is always a winner, the game remains exciting until the end: you can, for example, lose the first set with a difference of 20 points and win the second by a narrow margin in the shoot-out. In addition, beach handball emphasizes an individual, bodiless play, self-realization by trying out spectacular actions, and fair play. Last but not the least, the sand ground has a high appeal, and the beach atmosphere conveys a leisure and holiday image (see Fig. 2.11). However, this image does not contradict a serious and competitive sports alignment. Rather, beach handball offers the opportunity to clearly distinguish between pure fun events and targeted competitive sports. Both have their justification and significance in beach handball and are supported by the beach handball scene.

Although competitions are held separately by age and gender, there is nothing wrong with men and woman training together to prepare for competition. As the lack of physical contact cancels out men's natural mass and strength advantages, training sessions can easily be performed across genders (see Fig. 2.12). Children and young people can also be integrated into joint training with seniors more quickly than in indoor handball, for example.

In addition, the discipline of beach handball is characterized, above all, by its internationality and mutual respect. Despite the widespread lack of professional

Fig. 2.11 Holiday feeling at beach handball (Photo: Alex Gehrer)

Fig. 2.12 Cross-gender base training in beach handball

courts in beach handball, it is not uncommon in competitive sports and tournaments for a team to be made up of players from several nations (sometimes from different continents). Even if the communication is mostly in English, the game of beach handball itself seems to be an international language that connects people, regardless of their origin, religious background, or gender.

In conclusion, it is important that the claim "Beach handball is fairer than other handball disciplines or other sports" would not do justice to these disciplines and games. Handball is generally considered to be a sport in which fair play and mutual respect are highly valued. These aspects find a special expression in beach handball and are proudly embodied by all the athletes involved.

Advantages of Beach Handball for Kids and Beginners

The advantages of the beach handball sport for children and handball beginners are presented here. Furthermore, we explain the effect of the rules on the sport enjoyment of kids or handball beginners by presenting some principles of coaching and developing game forms or training practice.

Advantages of Beach Handball

In first place is certainly the beach handball game equipment. Children and young people in particular, but also beginners, often have problems gripping the ball in various sports (especially indoor sports). This difficulty does not apply to beach handball with the light and easy-to-grip PVC ball (see Fig. 2.13). In addition, the light ball takes away the fear of defending the ball.

Various advantage situations when playing in attack allow even supposedly underperforming players get goal throws. The goalkeeper position, which is often neglected and unpopular among children and beginners, has been greatly enhanced both by the simplified defence against the ball and by double scoring when throwing a goal.

Fig. 2.13 The easy-to-grip PVC ball simplifies the game play

Fig. 2.14 The sand leads to more confidence in handball actions

The risk of injury is much lower in beach handball than in other sports (especially indoor sports). For example, twisting one's ankle in the sand is generally not possible; there have already been numerous sports medical examinations on this. So, children and beginners have more confidence in the sand (jumps, dropping, etc.) (see Fig. 2.14).

Ultimately, fun and self-fulfilment also are increasingly important in sports. After all, it is precisely children and young people who find their values and lifestyle in a fun sport. Their expectations of sports for fun, leisure time enjoyment, excitement, action, and communication seem to be fulfilled by beach handball.

In summary, the following advantages of beach handball for children and beginners can be identified as follows.

- Physical contact-free/reduced play diminishes fears when entering the sport of handball.
- The soft surface reduces fears of falls.
- The ball is easier to grip: its properties make throwing/passing and catching easier.
- The smaller playing field and the smaller number of players on the field reduces the group tactical decision-making options and, thus, ensures fewer intense team demands.
- For the goalkeeper, the fear of body hits is also reduced by the softer ball.
- Failing in the goalkeeper's position has a lesser role because every goal-keeper can/should join in the attack and can, therefore, also have success in the attack.
- The permanent numerical advantage in attack allows a more attack-oriented offensive game.

(continued)

- The desired creative approach of the game, the sand, and the soft ball allow more spectacular actions even for inexperienced players.
- The structure of the game creates a higher density of events.

Sports-Related Enjoyment Principles

As described, beach handball has some significant advantages. The complex set of rules of the sport of beach handball can still seem very overwhelming for children and beginners. A simple reduction of the set of rules and, thus, a simplification of the game, is not sufficient to use it, especially for children. Rather, children's motivational and emotional needs should be explored. A set of rules and game forms can now be designed around these needs, which approximate the target game and, thus, function as the official set of rules.

The focus of these considerations should be the children's enjoyment with the sport. This enjoyment is directly linked to the level of participation in a particular sport. If it is possible to play game forms in which children experience a high level of enjoyment, they will show strong participation in the sport and, consequently, increase participation in beach handball. If the level of enjoyment with the training and game forms is too low, the likelihood that children will continue to play the game also decreases. However, the aim should be, with the correct control of the training content and training methods, not only to teach children as many beach handball skills as possible, but also to inspire them for lifelong participation.

To allow sufficient sports-related enjoyment for intensive beach handball participation, rules and guidelines for game and exercise forms should be planned and implemented with certain methodological principles taken into account (see Fig. 2.15).

Fig. 2.15 Sports-related enjoyment in beach handball (Photo: EHF)

The Principle of One's Own Competence Perception

A relevant factor in promoting sports-related enjoyment is giving children the opportunity to experience and exercise their own competences. If a pass to a teammate or a goal throw succeeds, the child feels a positive perception of competence, which will lead to greater enjoyment.

If only failures occur in the passing game or goal throwing, there will be little or no enjoyment. However, playing and practicing in a way that all actions are successful is also not positive, as boredom quickly occurs without any challenges, and there is then a lack of requirement character. Exercise and game forms should, therefore, be designed in terms of content and method so that the children can positively perceive their skills in more than 50% of all activities. In addition, exercise and game forms should be designed in such a way that the density of actions is very high (e.g., in goal throwing training, at least one action per minute per child).

If two teams play a game for 6 min against each other, at the end of the game 50% of the participants have a positive perception of competence (the winners) and 50% of the participants have a negative perception of competence (the losers). However, if you play this game in three sets (3 × 2 min) and score each set with a match point (see rules), there are also players from the winning team at the end who have a negative perception of competence. Within the game with the set structure, there is a probability that the losers have also won at least one set and so even temporarily have had a positive perception of competence. It is, therefore recommended, to always play game forms in a structure with several sets.

The Principle of the Specific Perception of Movement and Action

Monotony and extremely low or no pressure can quickly lead to a decline in sports-related enjoyment. Taking into account the principle of competence perception, a variable, and occasionally overwhelming, perception of movement and action is positively linked to sports-related enjoyment.

If a child has mastered the spin shot, future exercise and game forms should be designed in such a way that this spin shot is carried out under variable conditions of movement and action and, accordingly, permanently represents a specific sense of action for the child. Failure from excessive demands of complex variations is not necessarily negative and can promote a special sense of movement: such failure just must not be permanent (<50%).

The sand ground helps create a special perception of movement and action, which by itself leads to permanent variation and always brings new, unpredictable challenges. But even the sand can be manipulated in a targeted manner to increase this variation (e.g., smooth, not smooth, moisture content).

The weather conditions can also be used in a pointed manner. Strong wind, rain, or a low and blinding sun do not have to lead to an interruption of the training. Given the principle of the specific perception of movement and action, these conditions can be used effectively to promote the specific perception of moving and acting.

The Principle of Social Support and Interaction

If children feel social support within a group (e.g., people help each other) and a diverse interaction is possible (verbal and nonverbal), the sports-related enjoyment increases. Isolated forms of exercise offer fewer opportunities here; game forms or playful forms of exercise always lead to positive forms of social support and interaction. The interaction can be further strengthened through game forms with frequent independent substitutions and replacements or frequent independent roles and function changes. The neutral counting of the score (e.g., if a team scores a point, the whole team must shout their score out loud) greatly promotes aspects of interaction and social support. In shoot-out situations as a form of competition or training, such social support is particularly noticeable and can also be further fostered (e.g., all players cheer on their goalkeeper). Carrying out game forms selectively without verbal communication encourages the children to communicate nonverbally even more. This practice also promotes an awareness of social interaction and support and consequently also increases the sports-related enjoyment.

The Principle of Physical Activity and the Change in Intensity

Physical activity that sets the cardiovascular system in motion is positively linked to sports-related enjoyment. Games and game forms create this activity by themselves because of their inviting nature. Here, however, monotony, very long, low-intensity, or very long, high-intensity actions should be avoided. Physical activity becomes noticeable and effective with sports-related enjoyment when it is designed in an alternation between high-intensity movements and phases of rest. These changes in intensity also bring up the level of the games and game forms. However, they can be accelerated in a more targeted manner. Game phases should be short and an informal principle ("we want to play fast") can increase the intensity of these actions. Frequent substitution (e.g., the block change principle) leads to short, high-intensity phases in combination with short phases of rest and recovery.

The Principle of Autonomy

The level of sports-related enjoyment is also linked to the children's feeling of being able to act autonomously. The more autonomous the children feel, the more they believe that they are making their own decisions independently and not controlled by others, leading to them associating experiences of success with their own actions.

This principle should be integrated into the planning of exercises and games in such a way that as few "if-then" rules as possible are established. The children should be free to decide as often as possible whether they want to play the ball to the left or right, whether they finish with a normal shot on goal or with a spin shot.

In free game forms, this autonomy must be promoted in such a way that the scope of tactical rules is kept to a minimum (see Fig. 2.16). The instructions of the coach play a major role here. While an instruction like "if you get the ball from the left, you have to play it to the right" has a negative effect on the feeling of autonomy, an instruction like "if you get the ball from the left, look what options you have" gives more freedom of action here.

Fig. 2.16 Free and autonomous play in children's beach handball

In exercise forms in which abilities and skills are trained in isolation, however, a feeling of autonomy can also be increased through the degrees of freedom in action. If the goal throw from the spin shot is trained, the practitioner should, for example, be given the opportunity to expand the goal throw action into a pass action.

In general, children's sense of autonomy in the implementation of training or teaching sessions can be controlled in such a way that they are selectively included in the design of the rules (e.g., "Up to how many points do we want to play?").

Further Readings

Ehret A (1994) In: Steinle B (1994) Unterm Pflaster liegt der Strand. Handballmagazin 8:36–39
Gehrer A, König O (2008) Scouting in beach handball. Introduction into a qualitative analysis system. IHF Periodical, Basel
IHF (2021) Rules of the game. Beach handball. International Handball Federation, Basel
Tezcan B (2018) Beach handball world championships 2018. Qualitative analysis. IHF Periodical, Basel
Weichert W (1978) Handball. Unterrichtsmaterialien zur Sportlehrerausbildung für den schulischen Bereich. Hoffmann Verlag, Stuttgart
Zapardiel JC (2018) Propuesta de principios metodológicos para el entrenamiento técnico-táctico en balonmano playa. Federación Madrileña de Balonmano, Madrid

Basics of Rules, Teaching, and Coaching to Start with Beach Handball

Contents

F. Fasold et al., *Beach Handball for Beginners*,
https://doi.org/10.1007/978-3-662-64566-6_3

Top Rules for Your Start

The entire set of rules for the sport of beach handball is quite extensive and extremely detailed, consisting of 61 pages. The IHF offers this set of rules for free as a download on its homepage. To simplify this extensive set of rules and to make it usable in training and lessons for the first implementation of the game, the top rules are presented here with benefit-focused adjustments and explanations. Further rules, especially regarding the course of the game, will be added in the course of the game series to introduce the game.

Play Fair!

Even if a set of rules is meant to establish formal rules, the beach handball set of rules contains the informal rule of fair play. This fair play cannot be assessed objectively, as it is always a normative aspect. This mandated fair play relates, above all, to the respectful interaction with the opponent's health, respect for the spirit and philosophy of the game, and respect for the game flow, which should never be broken by a deliberate violation of the rules. For the implementation of the set of rules, this means that all the decisions in case of doubt should be made from the point of view of fair play.

Game Time and Structure of the Competition

Beach handball is played over two sets that are evaluated independently. The length of these sets is 10 min each with a 5-min break in between. Winning a set results in a match point. The team with two match points wins the game. If each team wins a set, it is a draw and the game goes into a decisive set, the shootout. Possible final results in beach handball are 2:1 or 2:0; there is no tie. In the event of a tie after the end of the playing time of a set, the game continues until a "golden goal" is scored. The referee starts it with a high ball.

The length of the set can be adapted to the level of development and learning of a group, but the competition structure (several sets) should always be maintained. A shortening of the sets is recommended here; sets longer than 10 min are not recommended for beginners.

The Ball

The game is played with an easy-to-catch rubber ball, which for men weighs between 350 and 370 g and has a circumference of 54 to 56 cm. For women, the ball has to weigh 280 to 300 g and be 50 to 52 cm in circumference. Smaller balls can be used for children and youth teams. The use of soft, good grip method balls (street handballs) is highly recommended. This rule does not only apply to children and youths; a ball that is easy to grasp should also be used in the senior sector at a beginner's level.

Several balls (at least three) should be available for each game, with the unused balls lying in reserve centred behind the goals. If a ball goes far out of bounds, fetching this ball would lead to a long interruption of the game. A reserve ball should be used so that the game can continue quickly.

The Playing Field and the Goals

The playing field is 27 m long and 12 m wide. In addition to the width of the playing field, 3-m transition/safety zones should be available on both sides. The surface is prescribed as fine-grained sand that has a minimum depth of 40 cm. To mark the playing field and goal area, two outer goal lines, two side-lines, and two goal area lines are required. As in indoor handball, the goals are 2 m high and 3 m wide (see Fig. 3.1).

These playing field requirements are laid down in the internationally valid set of rules but can be adapted to the level of development and learning and also to local requirements. Beach handball can also be played on smaller playing fields or on sand that does not comply with the rules.

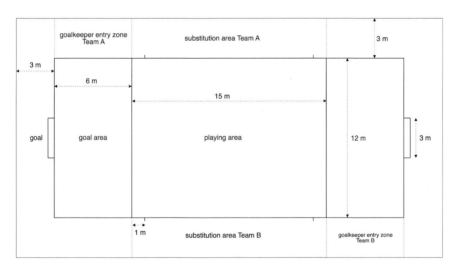

Fig. 3.1 Beach handball playing field

The Players

Beach handball is played with three field players plus a goalkeeper (marked by another shirt or jersey colour). Each team is assigned a substitution area (one side of the field) in which there is a maximum of six substitutes (see Fig. 3.2). The goal area of one's own team may only be entered by one's own goalkeeper. The players may substitute in their substitution area at any time, but only the prescribed number of players may be on the field at the same time (normally three field players and a goalkeeper). The goalkeeper can join the attack or be replaced by a specialist (also marked with a different shirt or a different jersey colour). All players play barefoot.

This number of players mentioned here corresponds to the rules, but this can be flexibly adjusted. A minimum of two field players plus one goalkeeper per team is recommended to implement the game idea. If more than 12 players (including goalkeepers) are available per team, it makes sense to divide the teams further or to play on a second playing field.

Playing the Ball

The ball may be played with hands, but all other parts of the body down to the knee can also be used to play the ball. The ball may be held for 3 s. After these 3 s, it must be played, thrown, or put in the sand. If the ball has been put down in the sand by a player, he/she may pick it up again once. Three steps may be taken with the ball in hand.

Fig. 3.2 Substitution area in beach handball (Photo: EHF)

All throws can lead directly to a goal (exception for referee throw/high ball). Diving for a lying or rolling ball is allowed. The goalkeeper may use any part of his body in the goal area to save the ball. He/she is also exempt from the step rule in the goal area. If the ball lies within the goal area, it can also be picked up by field players so long as they do not touch the goal area. The 3-sec rule and also the 3-step rule ares to be interpreted flexibly, especially for beginners. For beginners to count their steps or the seconds should be avoided.

The Referee Throw

Each set (and the "golden goal") starts with a high ball, executed by the referee (see Fig. 3.3).

The Goalkeeper Throw

After a goal there is no first-throw; the goalkeeper is allowed to bring the ball back into play with a throw/pass out of the goal area.

Scoring Points

A goal is scored with one point. If this goal is scored creatively or spectacularly compliant to the rules, it will be awarded two points. These spectacular goals include, in particular, the spin shot (throw after a 360-degree turn in the air around

Fig. 3.3 Referee throw (high ball) in beach handball (Photo: EHF)

your own body axis) and the Inflight (catching and throwing the ball while jumping). Goals by the specialist, the goalkeeper, and the 6-m penalty are always scored with two points.

For beginners, this regulation can and should be expanded to include other spectacular goals (e.g., throwing the ball through the legs or behind the back or a 270-degree spin shot).

The Shoot-Out

In the event of a tie after two sets, the "shoot-out" comes into play. Five players from each team take turns throwing after the goalkeeper's pass from their own goal area, taking into account the three-step rule, at the opposing goal. Both goalkeepers are located at their own goal line. The field player is at the intersection of the goal-area line and the side-line. After the whistle, the field player plays the opening pass to his own goalkeeper. As soon as the ball has left the hand of the player, both goalkeepers are allowed to move forward. The goalkeeper who takes the throw must, within 3 s, either throw directly at the opponent's goal or pass the field player running forward without the ball touching the ground. The field player must then receive the ball and attempt to score a goal by following the rules (see Fig. 3.4). If the field player or the goalkeeper who took the throw violates the rules, the action must be ended. If the defending goalkeeper violates the rules, a 6-m penalty throw is awarded. The winner is whoever has scored more points after five throws. If no decision has been made on both sides after five throws, the shoot-out will continue after changing sides until one team leads on points with the same number of throw attempts. Also in the shoot-out, creative and spectacular hits, as well as goals by the specialist, the goalkeeper, and the 6-m penalty throw, are awarded two points.

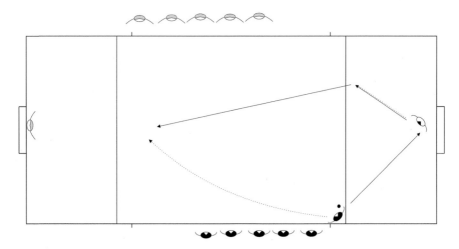

Fig. 3.4 Shoot-out in beach handball

Violations

A player can be suspended for unsportsmanlike conduct or physical contact that does not comply with the rules. Suspended players may be replaced or re-enter the field as soon as there is a change of possession between the two teams. The second suspension of a player causes disqualification (match penalty).

The currently valid indoor handball rules of the IHF apply, such as in beach handball, for example, preventing a clear scoring chance is punished with a 6-m penalty.

Game-Based Approach

Holistic-Analytical Approach
A game-centred approach is chosen to introduce the sport of beach handball. This approach cannot be assigned to a single method concept. Rather, it makes use of common method concepts that are established in general sports mediation. In summary, however, this can be described as a holistic-analytical approach. The implementation of the game idea is always paramount. At the start, the game requirements are minimized to such an extent that the game idea can be implemented even without any significant prior experience. This implementation is permanently analysed and optimized with game and exercise forms, and the game is further developed until it can be started independently under the conditions of the (internationally) applicable rules, played smoothly, and restarted in the event of interruptions.

The Concept of the Game

At the beginning of this methodological approach, an understanding of the game concept should be defined, which is not expressed through formal rules but primarily reflects the informal norms of how the game should be played. This concept of the game can be flexibly adjusted. Here, however, a view is recommended according to which the game should be played wisely, fairly, healthily, creatively, and dynamically. These standard categories themselves are to be explained with a group of athletes at the beginning and taken up again and again.

The Game Phases and Game Tasks

Different game phases and different tasks that are necessary for the implementation of the game idea are represented and made possible according to the game conception in each game form. The different phases of the game with the associated tasks are shown in Table 3.1.

Table 3.1 Game phases and game tasks in beach handball

Possession of Ball	Game Phases			Primary Task Player (+ specialist in offense)	Goalkeeper
No	Goalkeeper	Defence		Reconquering ball	Save
Yes		Offense		Scoring	Scoring/ substitution
No		Transition	Offensive to defensive	Reconquering ball	Save
Yes			Defensive to offensive	Scoring	Game opening

Defence

The elementary content of defensive behaviour in beach handball is the game against the ball. Attacking the body of the opponent is neither permitted by the rules nor wise to include in the game forms and would not correspond to the standard categories of wanting to play fair and healthy. Regardless of the progress in the implementation of the game and regardless of the currently implemented game or form of exercise, all athletes must be informed that only the ball is attacked in the defensive game. Violations of this principle should also be reported by the athletes themselves in the interests of fair play and not only be regulated by the game master or referee.

Another basic element of defensive behaviour is defending while being outnumbered. This element is expected to be found in every game form and must be exercised as early as possible, as soon as a fundamental implementation of the game idea is successful.

Offense

The general element in offensive behaviour is playing for points and not for goals. In contrast to indoor handball, this has a strong influence on the cognitive component of decision-making behaviour. Each player in a goal completion situation must decide whether to take any action with one possible point or an action for two possible points. This game for points and the associated decision-making behaviour should, therefore, be found in all games and exercises as early as possible. According to the game concept, all athletes should be advised from the start that an attacking game should be played wisely on the one hand and dynamically and creatively on the other.

Equivalent to defensive play, another general element of offensive behaviour is attacking in numerical advantage, which should be trained as early as possible in the game and exercise forms.

Transition

The transition game after a change of possession is to be equated in its relevance with offensive and defensive play. In terms of a dynamic and wise approach to the game, it is desirable to use a changed possession of the ball (regardless of whether you have conquered the ball or conceded a goal) by transmitting from defence to offense in a way that you can take advantage of the opponent's poor transition behaviour from defence to offense. For transition from offense to defence, it is paramount to striving to prevent the opponent's desired advantages by changing quickly. The substitution of players is strongly linked to this transition behaviour. These elements should be implemented in every form of play and exercise as early as possible.

The Goalkeeper and Specialist Game

The specific tasks and roles of goalkeepers in defence against balls and specialists in the offense do not have to be explicitly discussed from the beginning. Saving balls that are thrown at one's own goal is part of the game from the start in all game forms, even if this only happens implicitly. The special role of the specialist can and should only come into play later in the conception without it being lost in this holistic approach right at the beginning. The decision-making behaviour as to whether one or two points can be achieved with a game action is implicitly discussed from the start, with the introduction of the specialist; this is only explicitly expanded a little later.

Match Points as Competition Structure

A prominent characteristic of the sport of beach handball is playing for the frequency of points in several sets up to a certain number of match points (two for a win). This characteristic fundamentally differentiates the game from indoor handball, which is played in a one-set structure and around the frequency of goals scored at the end of a defined playing time. Because playing in sets and for match points has an extremely relevant influence on playing behaviour from a psychological perspective, this should be reflected in the game forms as early as possible.

Attack Trains Defence, Defence Trains Attack

If the game phases and primary tasks shown in Table 3.1 are implemented in the game forms, regardless of the level of the game and the number of formal rules, in the interaction of attack and defence game in the sense of the holistic approach, all skills and abilities required in the game are always trained instantly. It is important to include the respective norm categories of the game concept, even if they are not explicitly discussed in the current game form. If a game form is played in which the attack behaviour is to be improved, the norms for the defensive game (rule-compliant, wise, fair) are to be demanded at any time.

Organization of a Training Session

Because beach handball is mainly played outdoors, several things have to kept in mind to prepare the field and the athletes to have a healthy and safe time. Furthermore, in line with a goal-oriented practice and play, the methods and content of a training session should be the focus of a specific topic. This topic or elements of this topic should be integrated in every part of the session. In general, we provide a structure of following training parts: warm-up, practice and play, game, cool-down, and free practice time.

Preparing for Practice

Because beach handball is played outdoors and the play courts are exposed not only to the weather but also to different types of pollution, it is necessary to check the playing area before every game or training session. Garbage, glass, stones, or any other pointed objects must be removed. The sand often covers such impurities, so the entire playing area should be checked with a rake before training. The anchoring of the line systems and the goals should also be checked; the rule of "safety first" applies in all areas.

In the case of extreme heat and strong sunshine, sufficient breaks must be planned and the hydration of all those involved (including trainers) must be adequately guaranteed. Breaks should be held in the shade; if there are no shady spots available at the beach, these must be created with a mobile pavilion and/or parasols. Sunstroke or dehydration are absolutely avoidable and superfluous phenomena, which quickly take away the fun of beach handball, especially when working with children and beginners.

In addition to adequate sun protection for the skin with sunscreen, headgear can also be worn during training. Headgear is only permitted to a limited extent in competitions, but headgear may be mandatory during breaks in training and competitions to protect against the sun (see Fig. 3.5). Sunglasses should not be worn during training and are also not permitted in competition. During breaks, however, it is advisable to wear sunglasses to protect your eyes.

If the sand is too hot, it can be cooled down by watering it. However, this is not recommended in terms of environmental protection and the conscious use of water as a resource. Beach socks made of neoprene or fabric can protect your feet from sand that is too hot. According to the rules and regulations, these are not permitted in competition but can be used in training.

If the temperatures are very cold, especially the feet should be protected with neoprene socks. In addition to wearing long sportswear, this is the best way to protect the body from hypothermia.

Strong winds can influence training and the game but do not necessarily have to lead to an interruption of training so long as the safety of all participants is

Fig. 3.5 Sun protection by wearing headgear

guaranteed. Different weather conditions are part of the outdoor beach handball and should, therefore, also play a role in training.

In the event of a thunderstorm, every training session and game must be stopped immediately. Continuous rain also makes playful training practically impossible, but it can be used to train coordinative aspects (e.g., passing and catching wet balls). Light showers or drizzle naturally prevent competitions but are not a reason to forego games or training.

As beach handball facilities do not always have the equipment of handball halls, it should be ensured that first-aid measures can be implemented (a first-aid kit on site). A certain amount of still water to wash sand from eyes or injuries should also be available on site.

In addition to their training equipment (ball, clothing, sun protection, drinking water), the players should always have a small towel with them, which can be used to remove sand. If showers are available on site, they should not be unnecessarily contaminated with sand to conserve resources.

Structure of the Training Session

Warm-Up
Each training session should start with a warm-up part. The warm-up should not be purely considered as a physical preparation for the following exercise; rather, it should also contain the preparation for cognitive abilities (perception, anticipation, decision making) on a motivational and emotional level.

Fig. 3.6 Mobilization in the preparation phase with adults

Because dynamic movements (running, jumping) in the sand immediately demand a high-intensity action, the session should not start on a muscular level. It is recommended to set the start with three stages.

– (A) Mobilizing and strengthening exercises (air squats, easy jumps with one-legged landings, lunges, dynamic stretching) that can be performed in one place lead to a first warm-up of joints and muscles (see Fig. 3.6).
– (B) Physical activation through running techniques in all directions (forwards, backwards, sideways), and jumping techniques such as passing games in motion can be used for further activation after the mobilization stage.
– (C) Subsequently, cardiovascular load can be increased with small games (playing tag, zone games, relay competitions), which should always be performed with a ball. The small-sided games also activate cognitive abilities. Elements of the following session (e.g., catching, spin shot, inflight passes, diver blocks, footwork) can already be integrated into these types of play.

The warm-up course should be designed depending on the age group or performance level. If you train with pre-pubescent children, it is possible to begin directly with small-sided-games (phase C). The more advanced the physical development, the sooner phase A and phase B should proceed.

Goal-Oriented Practice and Play
In the main training phase, exercises and play forms should be carried out in combinations that are as effective as possible. Effective does not necessarily mean following a classic principle of going from easy to difficult; sometimes it is also advisable to integrate a very complex form of play or exercise right at the beginning.

Learning processes can be stimulated selectively with targeted excessive demands. Even though training forms with features resembling the game should be preferred because of the variable demands of beach handball, phases in which the pure practice of certain technical-tactical elements is paramount can also be used. However, these forms of exercise should at least be adapted to the spatial conditions of the game (e.g., the practice of passing and catching should not be carried out in isolation but in the typical playing position).

As the shoot-out with all its characteristics is a elementary part of the game, it should be taken into account in every training session in the exercise or play phase. The same applies to the goalkeeper's game. The goalkeepers should not only be on the goal but also be given the opportunity to (further) develop their skills and abilities in every part of the training sessions with goal-oriented tasks.

Game

A target game towards the end of the training session is not always necessary, but it offers a nice closing. The newly learned skills and abilities can be tested in a mock competition. From a motivational point of view, such a target game is also enjoyable for all athletes. If not enough players are available for a normal game, the target game can also be reduced to its basic game form.

However, it is relevant that target games are always carried out resembling the real competition, meaning that it always makes sense to play over two sets and a shoot-out. Serval sets or shoot-outs can also be played, but one-set games (e.g., 1×5 min), as is usual in indoor handball, should be avoided. In game forms close to competitions, it is always advisable to follow the structure of the real competition to train for pressure situations and simulate decision making in training.

Cool-Down and Time for Individual Training

The beach handball game always includes creative and individually designed opportunities for action and play. Towards the end of a training session, it is advisable to give each athlete a few minutes to work individually on their abilities and skills, and this can always be combined with a cool-down phase. According to the ages of athletes, a gymnastics-based end is conceivable, but the use of breathing or relaxation techniques also helps to bring an intensive training session to a comfortable end.

Basic Coaching Cues

The profile of a sport coach is generally a very complex one, and this also applies specifically to the profile of a beach handball coach. The competencies that are required to meet such a coaching profile are relevant not only for the

(continued)

beach handball coach but also for teachers or trainers. However, the main difference in the roles of a coach or teacher lies in the objective; one person wants to create a successful competition with his/her athletes, the other wants to convey knowledge and values with his/her teaching. The development of the personality of the athlete or student can be found in both roles. In pure competition coaching of a coach, success cannot always be quantified in terms of winning or losing, especially from a pedagogical perspective. As described, many competencies have an important role in all areas of teaching beach handball, and these competencies are explained here as general competencies and coaching cues.

Design and Implementation of Training and Teaching Sessions

The implementation of training and teaching sessions is the primary work area for a teacher, but this training process is also the most time-intensive task for a coach. In both roles, the task is to achieve optimal personal and athletic development of the athletes with the best possible individually coordinated teaching or training content. In addition to expertise in the field of the beach handball game (e.g., knowledge of game ideas, rules, structures), scientific training competencies (e.g., load control, the effect of training stimuli) should also be considered. Comprehensive pedagogical and psychological competencies in a coach (e.g., empathy, openness, structure, and organization) are just as necessary as knowledge of the effects and impact of instructions and criticism. The ability to act, especially concerning improvisation skills, the skill to quickly and flexibly adjust training forms creatively, is constantly required in the mediating roles in beach handball. In particular, the dynamics and the open conditions of a sport challenge these skills, and there are no patent remedies here.

Methods
The area of methodology mainly includes *how* to carry out training and teaching sessions, which methods can be implemented, and how they differ. Not only must game forms from exercise forms be differentiated to impart game-specific skills and abilities, but also these must be planned concerning physical load. Knowledge of methods of athletic training and how they work is also relevant. The use of aids, such as video feedback systems or training materials (different balls, air bodies), also requires methodical competencies.

Didactics
In this process, the didactics primarily describes the *what* to fill the corresponding methods with content that is effective for learning. When asked about the *what,* it should always be related to the game and the skills and abilities required in the game. Training content that cannot be found in the game is primarily irrelevant. However, if certain content is to be initiated, prepared, or even provoked, there is nothing to

prevent it from deviating in a targeted manner. Concerning the content, it is important to know the feasibility at the respective game level. Logically, a beginner needs different content than an advanced player.

Instructions

True to the saying "One Picture is Worth Ten Thousand Words," learning paths can be effectively and efficiently controlled using analogies or metaphors. Rules of movement or action explained in detail create a great deal of knowledge among the athletes; but these explanations sometimes make implementation more difficult because too many details can create excessive demands. Analogies, metaphors, or images simplify the learning processes for the athletes.

This type of instruction strongly directs the athletes' attention and, thus, has a strong influence on their actions. An instruction such as "make sure your elbow is higher when you throw" draws the athlete's attention to his/her own body. An externally placed attention "throw the ball over the height of my arm" leads to the same training target but directs the attention away from the body of the athlete. This external instruction facilitates learning.

Instructions in connection with attention also have a strong influence on the perception of the players. An instruction such as "If you get the ball from the left, you play it in the right-wing position," draws the attention strongly to an action which, in that moment, would possibly inhibit a better pass station (e.g., pass to the line position) to not be noticed. Open instructions are better: "If you get the ball from the left, see what options you have." Here the attention is directed more widely and the athlete will perceive more options independently (see Fig. 3.7).

Fig. 3.7 The quality of instruction is directly connected with the success of learning

Feedback

Before the feedback, the athlete should have the opportunity to reflect on his/her own action first and only then should the coach get involved. Verbal (but also nonverbal) feedback should, therefore, be given about 5 to 10 s after an action. In a short period, the athlete should now be able to internalize this feedback by repeating the action. This repetition should be possible within 60 s after the feedback so that the chances to forget are minimized.

Brain-Adequate Coaching

Based on the aspects mentioned, and some additional features, some coaching cues can be formulated concerning the coach's behaviour. These coaching cues also relate to the management of training and teaching sessions and also for competitions. They are set up in a way that optimal information processing can take place for the athletes.

Use of Positive Language

In terms of targeted reframing, negative terms can be converted into positively associated words and language (see Fig. 3.8). This way, "mistakes" can turn into "potentials", and defeats can lead to development. This is not always easy and requires an intensive and sometimes also planned examination of your own language.

Use of Simple Language

Technical terms or complex expressions should be avoided. The language chosen should be specific but as simple as possible. Because you often speak to many different athletes at the same time and each of these athletes can interpret and

Fig. 3.8 Positive language in coaching (Photo: EHF)

perceive the selected language differently, it is sometimes helpful to define certain terms. In the sense of a dictionary, it can be clarified what exactly is meant by a certain statement or a term.

Reformulate "Don't" Messages Into Active Guidelines for Action

"Don't always throw the ball low" becomes "throw the ball up." 'Don't' messages are difficult for the human brain to process, especially under stress. Concrete and active guidelines to act, however, are good and more expedient. These 'don't' messages cannot always be avoided. Even if they are uttered, the situation can be optimized with an active mandate to act immediately afterwards.

Keep the Amount of Information Short and Concise

Even if there are multiple considerations to be optimized, they cannot all be improved at once. It is, therefore, important to reduce instructions and feedback to the smallest possible amount that is understandable for the athlete. Things that could not be discussed do not have to be neglected altogether; there are opportunities to address them at a later point in time.

Staying Rational But Also Showing Emotions

In coaching (in competition as in training), calm should be maintained, the actions should be rationally evaluated, and the next actions should also be planned logically. Emotions can complicate these processes. However, emotions can also be very helpful. A positive emotional outburst of the coach about a successful action in training not only anchors this action more strongly in the mind of the executing player and makes it more effective in learning, but all other players who have seen this action will see the reaction to it positively and learn from it (see Fig. 3.9).

Fig. 3.9 Emotional coaching (Photo: EHF)

However, emotional outbursts wear out and lose their effect if they are used in excess. Purely rational coaching can also seem boring. A healthy mix of both will prove to be the most effective in fostering learning.

Targeted Praise

Pronounced praise or nonverbal praise via an affirmative clap further reinforces the effect of positive action. But, praise loses its effect if it is used in excess. Therefore, praise should always be targeted. It should also have temporal proximity to the action (within the first 5 s) to directly reinforce the positive emotion that occurs.

Targeted Criticism

Criticism may also be expressed, but this should also only be used occasionally and in a targeted manner. A critical statement should always be accompanied by a note to the athlete that he/she has to look for a solution to the point of criticism. If the athlete fails to do this, the coach has to suggest a solution.

Name Names and Make Eye Contact

The athlete should be addressed personally, by name, whether as instructions, feedback, or praise. Eye contact should also be established with the player when speaking to him/her. This practice helps to increase the attentiveness of the athletes and bind them to the coaching instruction (see Fig. 3.10).

Fig. 3.10 Address athlete personally by name and eye contact

Strengthen the Feeling of Autonomy

The athletes should be involved in the design and implementation of the training content and the search for solutions for problem areas. In a Socratic approach to conversation, the coach primarily acts in a questioning role: What would the solutions be? How could we play something? If the athletes manage to find the solutions and learning paths themselves, their sense of autonomy strengthens. Autonomy in thinking and acting is linked to an improved learning process on both a motor and a cognitive level.

Game Positions and Game Functions in Beach Handball

The changed number of players and playing area cause game position names that are chosen in beach handball to differ from indoor handball.

In addition to the game positions in beach handball, game functions must also be named and considered relative to the method of counting points and the structure of the game.

The playing positions are shown in the various attack and defence formations established in beach handball in Figs. 3.11, 3.12, 3.13, 3.14, 3.15. Also, the game functions have been added, which will be explained again in the following sections.

Labelling the Game Formations

As in indoor handball, labelling of the formations with numbers is helpful. In beach handball it is commonly done in one or two lines in the offense formations, thus, just two numbers are needed. The first number of a formation label represents the number of players in the first line, always looking from one's own goal. Therefore, the second number represents the number of players in the second line. If a team acts in offense with three players in the first line and one player in the second line (from one's own goal), the label of this offense formation is 3:1. If a defending team acts with three players in the first line and zero players in the second line (from one's own goal), this formation is labelled 3:0. If a one-to-one defence against one player is used, this is labelled with 2 + 1. Further examples are presented in Figs. 3.11, 3.12, 3.13, 3.14, 3.15.

Specialist/Goalkeeper

The play function of the specialist (attack) is always reflected directly in the attack formation. The play function of the goalkeeper (defence) is of course only performed in the goalkeeper position.

The specialist and goalkeeper game function is exceptional in that every goal scored by him/her is rated with two points. The player who takes on this

(continued)

function will be marked with a different jersey colour than his/her teammates. Also, this player is the only one who is allowed to enter his/her own goal area. The goalkeeper rules apply to him/her within this goal area. On the field of play, the field player rules apply to him/her, except for the point rule.

This function can be carried out by a player who is used on the defensive as a goalkeeper and on the offensive as a specialist. However, combining the skills as an attacker and goalkeeper is very complex and difficult to learn, as the requirements are too different. It makes sense to have two players perform these functions. A player with special skills for the offensive acts as a specialist in attack and substitutes when the ball possession changes to the opponent. A player with special skills as a goalkeeper then substitutes. If their team regains possession of the ball, the goalkeeper changes again and the specialist comes in again.

Field Player
The function of field players is carried out by all other players on a team. One is not allowed to enter both goal areas and can only score two points, according to the official rules and regulations, with a spin shot, inflight, or 6-m penalty.

Switching Player
The function of the switching players is not directly reflected in the line-up; the function of these players relates to the use of field players in attacking or defending play (change in the possession of the ball).

Runner
The function of the runner is only taken by field players, who, in contrast to the substitute players, play in a defensive as well as an attack position and are not changed.

Substitutes
The function of substitutes relates to players who are not on the playing field, but who are on the score sheet and can be substituted.

All game functions can be changed at any time. However, if a field player and a specialist/goalkeeper change roles, the change in jersey colour must also take place.

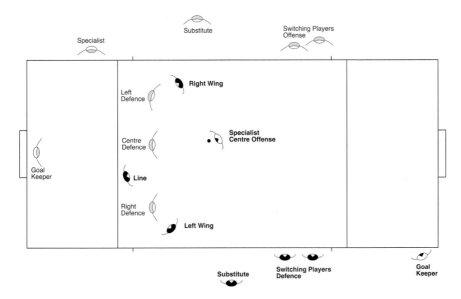

Fig. 3.11 3:1 offense with specialist on centre (in bold) against 3:0 defence

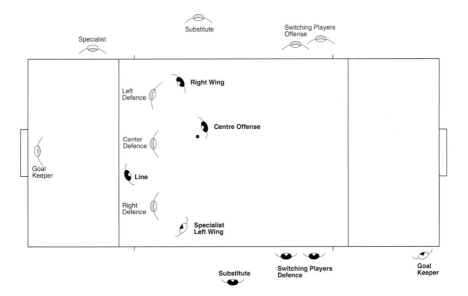

Fig. 3.12 3:1 offense with specialist on left wing against 3:0 defence

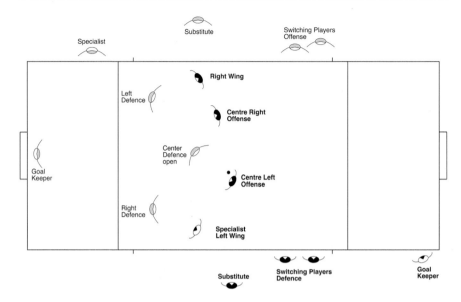

Fig. 3.13 4:0 offense with specialist on left wing against 2:1 defence with open centre

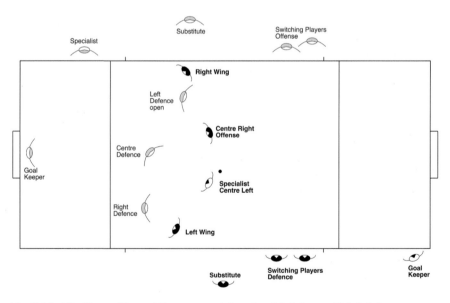

Fig. 3.14 4:0 offense with specialist on centre left against 2:1 defence with left defence open

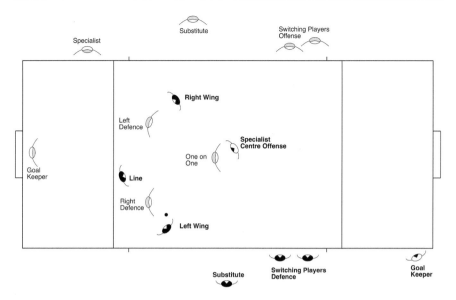

Fig. 3.15 3:1 offense with specialist on centre against 2 + 1 defence (one on one against specialist)

Further Readings

Bebetsos G (2012) Beachhandball from A to Z. The IHF Beachhandball handbook. International Handball Federation, Basel

Estriga L (2019) Team handball. Teaching and learning step-by-step. Agência Nacional, Porto

Griffin L, Butler J (2005) Teaching games for understanding: theory, research, and practice. Human Kinetics, Champaign, IL

Hapková I, Estriga L, Rot C (2019) Teaching handball. Volume 1: Teacher guidelines. Polic Press, Cairo

Hinkson J (2018) The art of motivation in team sports. A guide for coaches. Rowan & Littlefield, Lanham

IHF (2021) Rules of the game. Beach handball. International Handball Federation, Basel

Jeffreys I (2018) The WarmUp. Maximize performance and improve long-term athletic development. Human Kinetics, Champaign, IL

Passos P, Araújo D, Volossovitch A (2016) Performance analysis in team sports. Routledge, Abingdon

Just Play: From Beginner to Advanced in Seven Steps

4

Contents

Supplementary Information The online version contains supplementary material available at [https://doi.org/10.1007/978-3-662-64566-6_4]. The videos can be accessed by scanning the related images with the SN More Media App.

Based on the game idea of the handball discipline of beach handball, the presented game concept, and the internationally valid set of rules, a universal game series with seven content blocks has been developed that can be implemented with minimal effort (materials, etc.) for all age groups and across genders. This concept also applies regardless of the level of playing ability in the indoor handball discipline.

Within a few training sessions, this series of games provides a simple introduction to the game of beach handball (see Fig. 4.1). The speed at which individual aspects are introduced depends on the learning speed of the participants: if players make rapid progress, have quickly internalized new content, and acquired the skills and abilities to set the current game form in motion, to play smoothly, and to resume it in the event of interruptions, the next game form can be introduced. If there are too many interruptions, interventions and corrections often have to be made, or if the participants are permanently overwhelmed, one step back should be taken in the

Fig. 4.1 Just play beach handball with kids and beginners

series of games. The order of the game forms is not binding: it can be flexibly adapted and varied at any time.

Practice phases can also be used to improve specific skills and abilities with reduced requirements and later applied to game forms again. For example, if the participants have problems with the passing game over longer distances in the game form, a practice phase can be implemented in which only the passing game is discussed. If the participants improve in this, the game series should be taken up and continued.

The game series should generate and promote a high level of self-motivation as well as creative and dynamic game behaviour.

The individual learning contents in the seven levels of the game series are these

Step 1: Think openly

– Play freely and creatively on the sand and get to know the beach ball.
– Experience and implement the game idea.
– Get to know informal rules of gaming behaviour and the first formal rules of the game.

Step 2: Think fast

– Experience the speed and intensity of the game.
– Be quick in your head, be quick on your feet.
– Experience change as a central element of the game.
– Defend outnumbered to the offence.
– Defend without physical contact.

Step 3: Take care of the lines and areas

– Get to know the boundaries of the playing field.
– Be able to adapt one's own actions to space on the playing field.
– Play both defence and attack at the boundaries of the playing field.
– Get to know trick shots and use them consciously.

Step 4: Try beach handball

– Get to know mini- and ultimate beach handball.
– Experience the special roles of specialist and goalkeeper in a targeted manner.
– Get to know the set-counting method.
– Play beach handball according to official rules for the first time.

(continued)

Step 5: Focus on the shoot-out

- Get to know the shoot-out.
- Experience and train actions as a defender and goalkeeper.
- Experience and train how to act as a passing player and attacker.
- Be able to play shoot-outs according to official rules.

Step 6: Structure the game

- Get to know game positions and room division on the offense.
- Get to know game positions and room division on the defence.
- Experience the role of the runner function.
- Get to know the alternation of offensive and defensive players and use them in a targeted manner.

Step 7: Play beach handball

- Get to know other collective attack and defence formations.
- Get to know the effects of different formations on the game and the game tasks.
- Force the transition game.
- Learn specific tasks for goalkeepers and field players in the transition game.

Step 1: Think Openly

In the first game form of the series, the athletes should be made aware of the game idea, and the first confrontation with the ball and the sandy ground should take place. The game idea is to be developed from *simple goal throwing and ball conquering* to *scoring points through goals and conquering the ball*. Conquering the ball should be introduced in this game form in such a way that all athletes internalize that the game should take place without actively attacking the body of the opponent.

Informal Rules

The implementation of these aspects primarily takes place through the instruction of informal rules, which are not strictly enforced but are seen as standard categories and should be discussed together with the athletes. These informal rules are these: we

Fig. 4.2 Play free with a minimal framework of informal and formal rules

want to play wisely, we want to play fair, we want to play healthy for ourselves and our opponents, we only want to defend against the ball. If there are violations of these standard categories, the coach must address, explain, and discuss them again with the athletes (see Fig. 4.2).

An example of this could be the following situations:

We want to play wisely:

– An attacking player throws the ball at the goal despite being attacked by two opponents.
– Now the coach can interrupt the game and ask whether it makes sense to pass the ball if you are attacked by two defenders (one teammate, therefore, has to be free).

Formal Rules

In a progressive and interactive approach, small formal rules are added to this game form (each team only attacks one goal, the ball is only played by hand, step rule). These formal rules must be enforced, but also explained, by the coach, who is role playing as a referee.

An example of this could be the following situations:

The ball is only played by hand:

– An attacking player plays the ball by foot.
– The coach now interrupts the game, claims a change of ball possession, and explains the formal rule again, that the ball can only be played by using hands.

Both the informal and formal rules should only have a minimum coverage; all participating athletes should have a clear and free mind to be able to focus on the implementation of the game form.

Game Form A Two teams play against each other with one ball. The basic game idea of the sport of handball is implemented: throw goals and conquer the ball. Each team consists of a maximum of eight players. Each team attacks one goal and defends the other goal. The ball is only played by using hands. The team that first scores 5 points wins and receives a match point. The number of match points for a win can be freely chosen. The coach makes informal guidelines that the game is played wisely, fair, healthily, and only against the ball (see Fig. 4.3).

Introduction of the Step Rule

It can be assumed, in this game, that there are many violations of the formal step rule (3 steps with the ball allowed). It will often make sense to take more than three steps with the ball. The decisive factor when introducing the step rule, however, is the coaching instruction. If the coach instructs that from now on only three steps may be taken with the ball, the athletes will consciously start counting their steps when they are in possession of the ball, sometimes even looking at their feet. The attention and perception are massively distracted by the implementation of the game idea and a free dynamic game.

Informal instructions are more functional for introducing the game idea: "We want to pass the ball as often as possible," "We want to play fast," "We want to take as few steps as possible with the ball."

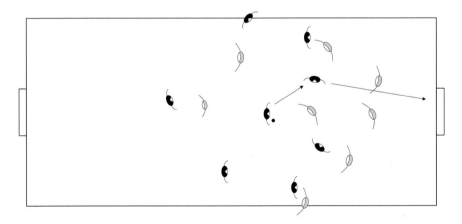

Fig. 4.3 Think openly in game form A

If there are situations in which an athlete takes more than three steps with the ball, the coach must interrupt the game. The ball possession should then not change; the athlete who committed the rule violation should be advised to take fewer steps the next time and/or to play the ball faster.

Using these informal tips, correcting one's own actions, and learning from the model (a teammate is corrected), all athletes quickly develop a feeling for the 3-step rule through an implicit learning process. If the athletes are ready to assess for themselves when they have taken too many steps (it will be recognizable by their body language), the step rule can be implemented according to the formal rules (change of possession in case of a violation).

Game Form B All rules (formal and informal) from game form A are adopted. Each team now has two goals (goal A and goal B) that they have to attack and defend. If a team scores a goal from an attack position (on goal B; Fig. 4.4), this is scored with one point. If a team regains possession of the ball, it can attack both goal A and goal B, but two points would be awarded for a goal in goal A. The attacking team then has to decide whether it is easier to score one point—the opponent will not defend goal B as intensely—or more difficult to score two points on goal A, which the opponent will defend more intensely. If the attacking team makes goal A, it receives two points. In the next attack, there would be two points for a goal in goal B.

The game idea of handball (throwing goals, conquering balls) is now adapted for the first time to the game idea of the discipline of beach handball to score points through a goal and conquer the ball.

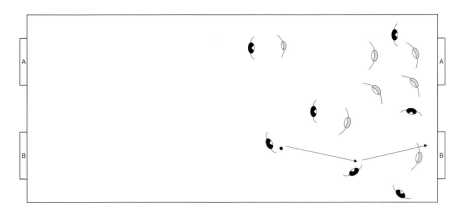

Fig. 4.4 Think openly in game form B

Game Form C The content and structure here are based on the previous game forms, but only one goal is played. The part of the game idea of *scoring points* is trained for by the fact that the throwers are free to choose whether they want to score one point with a simple throw or two points with a trick shot. Before the games, the coach lets the athletes determine which type of trick shot results in two points (e.g., throw behind the back, throw with both hands). The level of difficulty of the trick shots should be checked by the coach for the performance of the athlete.

Step 2: Think Fast

Beach handball places high demands on the athletes in terms of the speed of action, regardless of their level of performance. Primarily, this relates to the cognitive components of the speed of action: how quickly do I perceive something, how quickly do I make a decision, how quickly and how well I can anticipate. All these aspects are often decisive for success or failure. This cognitive speed can be overwhelming for the players. However, in simple game forms, the cognitive speed can be trained as well as with beginners.

The playful training of the speed of action is based on a simple norm, the block-change principle, which can be integrated into almost every game form of the game series and is illustrated below in two different game forms (see Fig. 4.5).

Fig. 4.5 Fast transition between defence and offense and fast substitution in beach handball

Another component that places high demands on the perception of the athletes and thus on the speed of action in beach handball is being permanently outnumbered in the defence game. This outnumbered defence should also be introduced in a playful way, building on the block-change principle.

Game Form A Based on the introduced rules in Step 1 and the skills and abilities acquired, two teams of eight players each play against each other. The aim is to throw the ball into the opponent's goal and regain the ball without body contact. A point regulation using trick shots can also be introduced.

There are always only four players from each team on the field, and four other players from each team stand in a designated substitution area. If a team scores a goal, all four players on the scoring team must substitute (see Fig. 4.6). Only substituted players are allowed to defend and prevent a quick attack on their own goal, which is now empty. The team that conceded the goal can switch quickly, take advantage of the alternate and substitute phase of the other team, and gain an advantage for a simple goal throw through a fast play.

The block-change principle means that if a goal is scored, all players of the successful team must leave the field collectively and a new block of players from their team must replace them. Only four players are allowed on the field at the same time. Thus, if only one player leaves the playing field for the substitution area, another player could take his/her place.

If a team plays with an unequal number, for example, a team with five substitutes rather than four (total, nine players), one player must remain in the substitution area

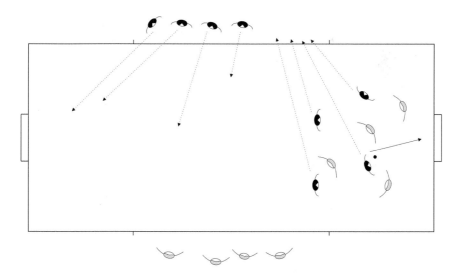

Fig. 4.6 The block-change principle in game form of "think fast"

at the time of the change. Similarly, if a team has only three substitutes (total, seven players), one player may remain on the field and is exempt from the substitution.

If the block-change principle leads to the problem that the game gets too fast and there are many throws at the empty goal one after the other, the speed can be reduced somewhat with additional rules (e.g., the ball must be passed twice before a goal throw).

Game Form B All rules and guidelines from game form A are adopted here. A player of the team that is not in possession of the ball is exempt from defensive duties. He/she must sit down in the sand next to his/her own goal. If his/her team wins the ball, he/she may stand up and integrate himself/herself into the offensive game as an attacker (see Fig. 4.7). If his/her team concedes a goal, he/she is the one who has to get the ball out of the goal and afterwards initiates the offensive game of his/her team with a pass.

> As an addition, this player can assume the role of the goalkeeper. However, he/she may only act defensively and not leave his/her goal line significantly.

Being permanently outnumbered in defence and having to determine the player who goes next to or in the goal not only demands and promotes the athletes' ability to perceive, anticipate, and make decisions, but also stimulates communicative and cooperative processes among the teammates.

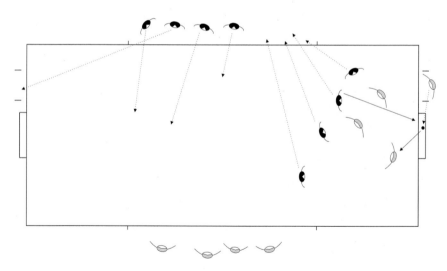

Fig. 4.7 Think fast in game form B with outnumbered defence (in defence, one defender sits next to the goal; in ball possession he/she may integrate himself/herself as an attack)

Both game forms should again have a competitive character in the form that several sets are played up to a predetermined number of points. First plays for time are also possible, but several short (e.g., 4 × 2 min) games should be played instead of one long set (8 min).

Step 3: Take Care of the Lines and Areas

The game forms presented in this chapter are intended to implicitly raise awareness of the boundaries of the field with the players, especially the side lines, goal lines, and the goal area. The game forms are chosen in such a way that during training the players have to deal with the lines and the distances to these lines in exercises similar to game situations, without an explicit focus being placed on them. A feeling for the correct distance of the court lines and the playing area (court, goal area, transition area) should be developed from offensive and defensive actions (see Fig. 4.8).

Game Form A All previously introduced rules from Step 2 remaining as they were, the court is now amended by side-, goal-, and goal area lines (see Fig. 4.9). The game is played in the court; a goal can be scored when a player from within the court passes the ball over the goal-area line to a teammate. The ball may no longer be passed within the goal area. The ball must be thrown directly into the goal, in consideration of the step rule, or, if that is not possible, passed back into the court via the goal-area line to any other player and, thus, released again. If the ball touches the ground behind the

Fig. 4.8 Awareness of the lines and areas as the next step in learning beach handball

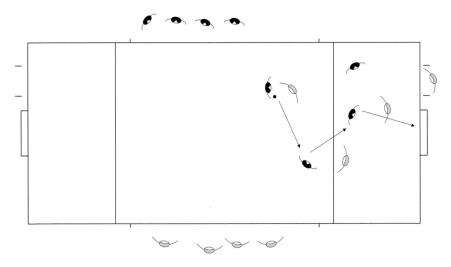

Fig. 4.9 Introducing and implementing field markings in game form A

goal-area line (in the goal area), the defending team gains the possession of the ball. Any number of players of one team may stay in the goal area at any time. The coach should now, in case of rule violations, explain how to deal with those:

a. If the ball goes out, there is a throw-in for the other team. A throw-in is taken by a player with one foot on the line.
b. If a player with the ball steps over the goal line, the possession changes. The game continues with a pass at the point where the mistake was made.

If a smooth game is underway and the rules are followed by the players with regard to the court lines and the goal lines, trick-shot rules can be introduced:

a. The player who catches the ball in the goal area gets two points with a goal scored from the spin-shot.
b. A goal scored by inflight also counts for two points.
c. Further goals scored creatively or spectacularly also counts for two points (e.g., throw behind the back, throw through the legs).

It is important to note the defensive playing style in all forms of play and variants. It is played in a healthy way (contact free and bodiless) according to the game concept, and only the ball is attacked.

Game Form B All previously introduced rules from the game form A with regard to the field markings (see Fig. 4.10) remain in play. A point can be scored by a player from the court with the ball in hand touching the goal area line with his foot. Three attackers play against two defenders but are only allowed to take three steps with the

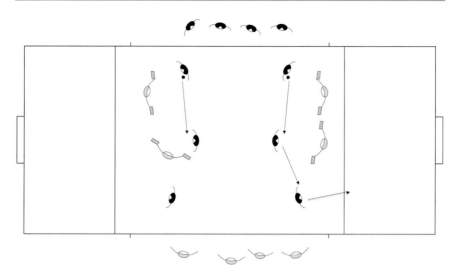

Fig. 4.10 Three versus 2 playing with the side- and goal area lines in game form B

ball. The defenders receive two shirts each, one for the right hand and one for the left hand. If the ball or the opponent with the ball is touched by the defending team with a shirt, the defending team receives one point. If the offensive team is able to put one foot on the goal line with the ball not being touched by a defender with the shirt, it receives one point. The team that scores a specified number of points that is determined at the beginning, wins (e.g., the one that scored five/seven/nine points first). The game could be played on both sides of the field.

Game Form C In the next game form, a point is scored when a player on the court passes the ball over the goal-area line to a teammate. The game is played in tied numbers (e.g., 4 versus 4). At any time, only one player from the attacking team and one permanent player from the defending team are allowed behind the goal-area line. As soon as the ball possession changes, a player from the defending team must go into the goal area. If the ball touches the ground behind the goal-area line (in the goal area), the defending team gains possession of the ball. In defence, the game is played in a healthy manner (contact-free and bodiless) and only the ball is attacked (see Fig. 4.11).

Game Form D In this game form, a point can be scored if the attacking team hits the post- or the crossbar with a throw (see Fig. 4.12). One fixed match ball is available for each team. The attacking team is always outnumbered. If the attacking team finishes the offensive play (by scoring or losing the ball), the thrower (or the player with the last contact to the ball) must then collect the ball and then go to the substitution area. He/she is responsible for getting himself/herself and the ball back into play for the next attack. If the defending team succeeds in catching the ball, they

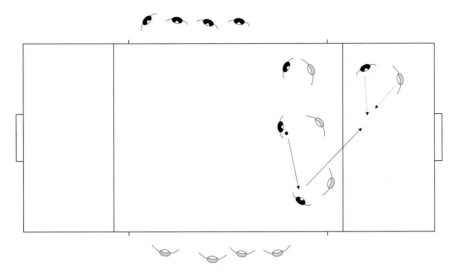

Fig. 4.11 Four versus 4 playing with the goal area and goal-area lines in game form C

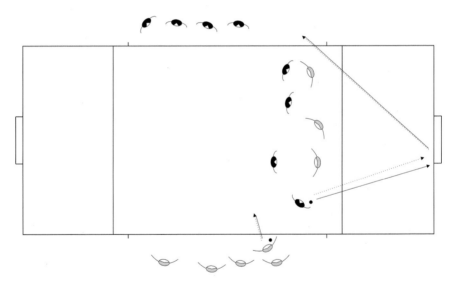

Fig. 4.12 4:0 offense against 3:0 defence: hitting the post or the crossbar with a throw in game form D

put it on the ground. The passer of the intercepted ball collects the ball and waits for the next attack in the transition area.

If a game is implemented smoothly and the rules are followed by the players, trick-shot rules can be introduced, similar to game form A.

Step 4: Try Beach Handball

In the learning sections Step 1 through Step 3, skills and abilities were acquired that made it possible to play the first beach handball games. So far, the special role of the goalkeeper in defensive play and that of the specialist in offensive play have been neglected. These two roles will be introduced through the mini-beach handball and ultimate beach handball game forms, and further beach handball rules will be progressively added. Following these two game forms, which for the children's level represent forms of competition for the U10 (Mini) and U12 (Ultimate) classifications, beach handball is played for the first time according to the official rules, but still very freely in terms of tactics and game action.

The game forms of mini- and ultimate beach handball have been adopted and modified from the framework of training concept of the German Handball Federation (2022), publications of the EHF, and Fasold and Gehrer (2019). It is important to remember that mini- and ultimate beach handball as a form of competition is always carried out in two sets and with a shoot-out. In this level (mini and ultimate) of the game series, the shoot-out does not yet have a role. The rules and structures of mini- and ultimate beach handball are aimed at picking up the skills and abilities of the athletes at their current level of performance and developing them further for future performances.

In these game forms, the athletes should apply the principles learned in the previous game forms and implement them together in a play-related manner. The athletes should

– Defend without body contact.
– Attack creatively and imaginatively.
– Know and use the playing field.
– Get to know the method of counting points.
– Change in the block (after a goal or loss of the ball) and, thus, to remain engaged and active in the game as a substitute at all times.
– Experience the special roles of goalkeepers and specialists.

Mini-Beach Handball

The game is played on a field of reduced size (e.g., 12×8 m, two goal areas of 5 m each) and a substitution area for each team along an entire side-line. Each team consists of (at least) eight players: four are on the playing field, and four are in the substitution area (more than four players are allowed here). One of the field players may enter the goal area and act as a goalkeeper (without marking by a different-coloured jersey). He/she may also join the attack after winning the ball. If a team scores a goal, all four players must substitute, regardless of where they are on the

Fig. 4.13 Instructions mini-beach handball (Photo: Alex Gehrer)

Fig. 4.14 Easy palpable ball (Photo: Alex Gehrer)

field. Also, while holding possession of the ball, each team may always substitute freely. The opposing team may continue to play immediately after conceding a goal with a goalkeeper throw from their own goal (see Fig. 4.13).

The game is played with a street handball (soft ball) (see Fig. 4.14). There should always be three balls close to the field (one as a game ball, two behind the goals as replacement balls).

The standard scoring method is used for counting points here. Every goal that the referee considers spectacular is awarded two points. This category includes, for example, spin shots (even without 360-degree rotations and a two-legged jump), inflight (also hit balls), throws from the frog jump, 5-m penalty throws, and throws from your own goal area. All other creative but successful attempts are also scored with two points (throw through the legs, behind the back, etc.).

A game is played over three sets with a predefined time (e.g., 3 × 5 min).

With regard to playing the ball, step limits, body contact, and all rules from the beach handball set of rules apply.

Ultimate Beach Handball

The game is played on a normal beach handball field (27 × 12 m). Each team consists of (at least) eight players: four are on the playing field, and four are in the substitution area (more than four players are allowed here).

Two of these players (one on the field, one in the substitution area) must be marked with a different colour and act as specialists. Only specialists are allowed to enter their own goal area and act as goalkeepers. The specialist may also intervene in the attack after winning the ball.

If a team scores a goal or there is a change of possession, all the three field players and the specialist/goalkeeper must substitute, regardless of where they are on the field. After a goal has been scored, the game can continue immediately with a throw-off from the goal.

The game is played with a size 1 beach handball. There should always be three balls close to the field (one as a game ball, two behind the goals as replacement balls).

The standard scoring method for counting points is used here as well. Every goal that the referee considers spectacular is awarded two points. This category includes spin shots (even without 360-degree rotations, but with a two-legged jump), inflight (also hit balls), 6-m penalty throws, and throws by specialists or goalkeepers from their own goal area.

A game is played over three sets with a predetermined time, but the time in the third set is significantly shortened to initiate the action of the shoot-out (e.g., 2 × 7 min + 1 × 2 min).

With regard to playing the ball, step limits, body contact, and all rules from the beach handball set of rules apply.

Beach Handball in Free Play

In the third game form in this chapter, all rules and structures are taken from the Ultimate game form. However, the rules for changing blocks are no longer in play. The teams can now decide for themselves how to make the substitutions. There are several options for this:

- If the ball is lost or after a goal is on the offensive, the specialist changes and a goalkeeper replaces him/her. All field players act as runners and then switch when they are tired.
- Goalkeepers and specialists are predetermined: only one player on the defensive acts as a goalkeeper, and only one player on the offensive as a specialist.
- The teams define initial substitution strategies to optimize their game (e.g., one player only plays offensive, leaves the playing field when the ball changes possession, and another player enters as a defensive player).

For the athletes to test themselves, it is important to play in short sets (e.g., up to 6 points, 4 min) and to allow the teams to discuss and adapt their substitution tactics and strategies in between. The coach should not instruct too much here but only act as a support and source of ideas.

Standbild Promotion Video for Mini- and Ultimate Beach Handball. (▶ https://doi.org/10.1007/000-6c1)

Step 5: Focus on the Shoot-Out

In the series of games from Step 1 till Step 4 the athletes acquire a certain playing ability, understand the game idea, and get to know about the special functions on the field (specialist, goalkeeper). The athletes are also familiar with the structure of the competition (playing for match points) by now, and only lack knowledge of the shoot-out. This shoot-out should be used immediately to decide a game when each team has won a set and the score is 1:1 in terms of match points.

Fig. 4.15 Shoot-out in beach handball

The shoot-out will be introduced as a competition, but methodical simplifications and changes will be created to reduce the level of overstrain of the athletes and to lessen the risk of injury.

For an isolated shoot-out action, the rules state that a shooter, along with a passer, competes against a defender (see Fig. 4.15).

The passer and the defender/goalkeeper must stand with their feet on the goal line to start an action, the shooter with the ball with one foot on the corner of the touchline-goal-area line. At the signal of the referee (whistle), the shooter plays the ball to his/her passer, who, and also the defender, are allowed to leave the goal line at this moment.

The shooter must now move forward in the direction of the other goal. The passer is released from the step rule in the goal area but is not allowed to leave his goal area. He/she may pass the ball but also throw it at the opposing goal.

The defender may act as a goalkeeper within his/her goal area, but may also leave his/her goal area to try to conquer the ball while following the rules.

During the entire action, the ball may only touch the sand when throwing a goal; if it falls into the sand during a passing game, the action is over.

A goal by the passer is scored with two points. A goal by the shooter is scored with one point; if he/she scores the goal with a spin shot or inflight, this is scored with two points.

Should the defender irregularly prevent the goal (foul or un-sportsman-like behaviour) he/she will be disqualified, and the attackers will be awarded a 6-m penalty.

The shoot-out action, according to the official set of rules, represents two levels of intensive demands for the beginners: (a) The passing game for shooters and passers, which often leads to errors under the pressure of the shoot-out; and (b) as the offensive action of the defender, he/she leaves his/her goal area to intercept the pass or to block the ball offensively. Because the attacking shooter does not see the defender running out, there is a great risk of injury here.

In the exercise forms shown next, these levels of overstraining should be reduced at the beginning, closer to the competition, and later brought closer to the official set of rules. Rule extensions should also target the offensive defence of the shoot-out situation, as this is an elementary part of the game.

The size of the playing field at the shoot-out should be adapted to the age. The shoot-out is always played on the field that was previously used for playing or training.

First-Steps in the Shoot-Out

Both teams take the normal shoot-out line-up. Every player of a team must compete as a shooter in the shoot-out. The order is fixed at the beginning. The passer is always the next shooter in this order. The defender from the other team is always the next shooter in the order of the other team. If a team is outnumbered, one player must act in the shoot-out twice.

At the beginning of a shoot-out action, the passer and the defender are not limited to the goal-area line; they are free to move in the goal area. But neither of them is allowed to leave their goal area, so the defender acts purely as a goalkeeper.

The ball may fall into the sand only once during a shoot-out action (pass of the shooter to the passer, pass of the passer to the shooter). A pass or catch error does not end the action immediately. Furthermore, if the ball was not in the sand before, the shooter may put the ball down once to approach the goal with another three steps.

The standard scoring method is used for counting points.

If there is a tie after each player of a team has had their turn, one player from each team competes in 1-on-1 until one team has the lead.

Increase the Level of Difficulty: Part 1

If the athletes succeed in showing high pass security in the first-steps of the shoot-out competition (90% of all passes arrive), the rule that the ball may fall into the sand once or the shooter may put it down only once; it can be lifted in the next step.

The procedure is the same as in the shoot-out attempts, but the tightening of the rules significantly increases the level of difficulty in the passing game.

Defend Offensively and Enable Coast-to-Coast Attempts

Because the running action of the defender playing an offensive game is a great risk of injury in the beginners' area, it should be initiated and trained in a targeted manner. If the athletes are confident in the passing game and shooting a goal despite the increased difficulty, the next step can be taken here.

The structure and order of the first-steps competitions remain the same, but the defender now starts on the goal-area line (see Fig. 4.16). After the start of the action, he/she can now decide whether to run back into the goal area or into the playing field to intercept or block the ball.

> The defender is responsible for the health of the shooter and must act in a completely contactless manner. If he/she touches the shooter even minimally, he/she will be disqualified, and the attackers will be awarded a 6-m penalty. The defender, therefore, is not allowed to provoke an offensive foul.

The passers can, at this stage, try more often to throw the ball directly at the goal. They have to watch the defender's behaviour closely and decide whether to throw the ball or pass it.

Increase the Level of Difficulty: Part 2

If all athletes gain confidence in running out (conquering the ball or blocks without physical contact), the passes arrive and if coast-to-coast attempts by the passers succeed, the level of difficulty can be further increased.

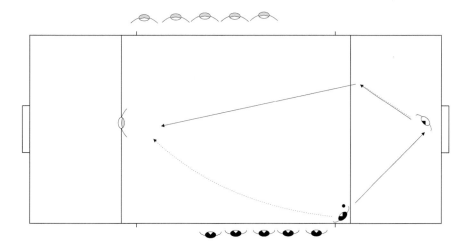

Fig. 4.16 Shoot-out with running out of the defender

The passer can now start at the beginning of the action, following the official rules, on the goal line. This increases the precision and situation pressure on passers and shooters.

In the next step, the defender must also start from the goal line at the beginning of the action. This increases the pressure of the situation for him/her too; under difficult conditions, he/she must decide whether to run out or stay in the goal area as a goalkeeper.

Shoot-Out According to the Rules

If the athletes can show a safe passing game, get into the shot safely, act as a goalkeeper, or defend offensively without physical contact, the official set of rules can be implemented.

The defender may now position himself/herself offensively in a way that the attacker commits an offensive foul. Here, however, the safety-first rule still applies; the defender is responsible for the shooter's health.

There are now only five shooters from each team, but in each action, the defender/ goalkeeper and passer can be freely chosen.

Step 6: Structure the Game

The game forms in Step 1 till Step 5 should be played very freely in terms of the game structure and the tactical guidelines. The collective requirements for the participating athletes should only be to play freely, use the space, and win the ball.

To develop the first tactical specifications for the defence, attack, and transition game (offensive to defensive; defensive to offensive), a holistic approach should be chosen. In this approach, target games are played, and the tactical specifications are integrated piece by piece until all athletes have a basic collective internalized tactical structure. Additionally, the athletes should become familiar with other game functions: the runners, the changing players (offensive players, defensive players), and the substitutes.

In terms of the methodology that tactical action in attack requires tactical action in defence, it is recommended to approach the tactical structure from the offensive perspective.

Make Optimal Use of Spaces in an Attack

A target game is played in which five players per team are permanently on duty in short sets (e.g., 3 min). Each team has a goalkeeper, a specialist, and three field players. The goalkeeper is a substitute for the specialist and vice versa. If a team wins the ball, the specialist replaces the goalkeeper and plays on the offensive. If the ball changes again, the specialist changes and the goalkeeper replaces him/her on the defensive (see Fig. 4.17).

The only target of the three field players on the defensive is to conquer the ball. In the offensive, they should be divided in such a way that one player occupies the right side of the playing field (right-wing position), one player occupies the left side of the playing field (left-wing position), and one player positions himself/herself on the line (line position). If this player is right-handed, he/she positions himself/herself at the left goalpost (viewed from his own goal), if he/she is a left-handed player, he/she positions himself/herself at the right goal post. The specialist occupies the centre (centre-offense-position) (see Fig. 4.17). This space division should be used again and again, especially at the beginning of an attack, but it should not be rigidly adhered to; changing and leaving the spaces is permitted at any time. This division of space is described as a 3:1 attack (see Fig. 4.18).

Many short sets should be played, and the players who are not among the five players involved are substitutes and are used permanently in the next set. Positions and functions should also be swapped between the sets in such a way that all players gain experience in different positions and different functions (specialist/goalkeeper).

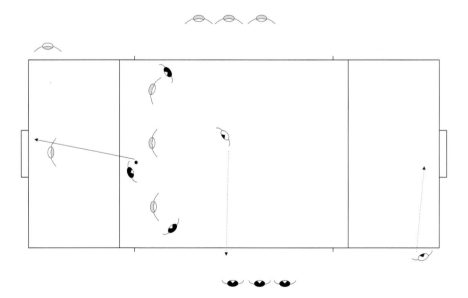

Fig. 4.17 Offensive play and the goalkeeper and specialist substitution

Fig. 4.18 Visualization could help the understanding of the game

Defend Against the Ball in the Space

If a division of space succeeds in attack and the players have gained confidence in taking and leaving the attack areas, as well as changing the goalkeeper and the specialist, the first collective specification for the defensive game can be made.

The basic requirement in the defence game remains that it is not the body of the opponent that is attacked, but purely the ball. This free defence requirement is now also spatially structured. All three field players position themselves on a line, one player occupies the right (defence-right-position), one player the left (defence-left-position), and one player occupies the central area of the playing field (defence-centre-position). The aim of the defence game is now to defend the ball when it is played in the respective defence area (see Fig. 4.17). This game plan is described as a 3:0 defence.

To facilitate the structuring of the game, the player who occupies the defence-right position plays the right-wing position in the attack, the player who defends the defence-left position plays the left-wing position in the attack, and players who occupy the defence centre position play the line position in the attack.

Get to Know and Use Alternation: Play with Two Runners

If it is possible to play both attack and defence in this simple spatial structure, the roles of the runner and switching players can be introduced. The runner function is performed by players who play a position both in attack and in defence. Switching players are players who are only used in the attack or only in defence. In addition to

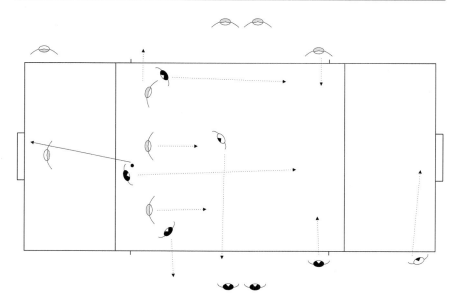

Fig. 4.19 Transition between offensive and defensive players: a new changing system with two runners

this, it must be explained that substitutes are the players who are not actively taking part in the game.

After the games for the introduction in a 3:1 attack against the 3:0 defence are played with three runners (all field players play both a defensive and an attacking position) and only the specialist and the goalkeeper can switch between offensive and defensive; another change can be introduced.

Six players now take part in the game: a specialist, a goalkeeper, two runners, a switching player for the defence, and a switching player for the offense. The field player positions that are furthest away from one's own transition area are played as runners (Team A: defence-left/-wing, defence-centre/-line; Team B: defence-right/-wing, defence-centre/-line). The position in one's own transition area (see Fig. 4.19, Team A: defence-right/-wing; Team B: defence-left/-wing) is occupied by two players. If team A takes possession of the ball on the defensive, the player switches to the defence-right position; in the attack, the other player on the offensive switches to the right-wing position (for team B on the other side) (see Fig. 4.19). If the ball possession now changes back to team B, the player on the right-wing position on the offensive changes again, and the player on the defence-right position changes in. The specialist and goalkeeper of both teams will change as they did in the previous games.

Force Alternation: Play with One Runner

If a safe substitution and exchange succeed in compliance with the rules in this position (only three field players may be on the field at the same time) and the game with two runners, another position can be changed, and the team can continue with one runner.

At this stage, there are seven players per team taking part in the game: a specialist, a goalkeeper, a runner, two switching players for the defence, and two switching players for the offense. According to the game with two runners, the attacking and defending positions are close to one's own substitution area. When the ball possession changes, the player in the line position in the attack also changes, and another player enters in the defence-centre-position. The game is now only played with one runner; this runner always occupies the attack and defence position that is farthest away from one's own changing area (see Fig. 4.20).

Many short sets should also be played in these forms of play, and all players should be able to gain experience in different positions and functions (runner, substitute player). Because playing as a runner is physically very challenging, one can also play with substitute players. The runner gets a break after a certain playing time and is replaced by a substitute. The function of the specialist can also be very physically challenging. Here, too, it is possible to act with substitutes.

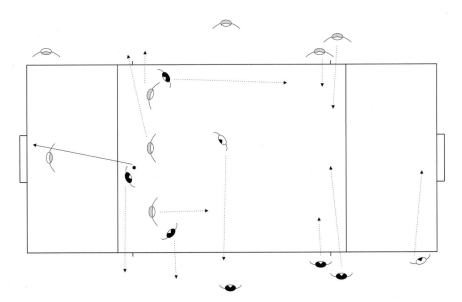

Fig. 4.20 Transition between offensive and defensive players: a new changing system with one runner

Step 7: Play Beach Handball

> Based on the skills acquired and the game knowledge through the game and exercise forms carried out in the further steps, all athletes should be able to start a beach handball game compliant with the rules, resume it in the event of interruptions, and be able to play with basic tactical structures.
>
> Target competitions should be played as close to the nature of the real game as possible. Games should always be played over two sets with the option to decide on the shoot-out. The length of the sets does not have to be 10 min; shorter sets can also be implemented, and the shoot-out does not necessarily have to be implemented with five shooters per team.

Defence and Offense

To increase tactical variability in the game and to expand game skills, further basic attack and defence formations are presented here that challenge and thus train tactical behaviour. Here, the interaction between attack and defence behaviour applies. If the defence formation changes, changed attack actions are required; if the attack formation changes, changed defence actions are required.

The 2:1 Defence Formation
In the 2:1 defence formation, the player in the defence-centre position moves offensively and aggressively to a front line (see Fig. 4.21). The defence, consequently, increases the pressure to act on the attacking position of centre-offense and makes it more difficult for the attack to pass the game across the board. Thereby, the defence also opens up the central space on the line, which requires new options for the attack.

Defence Pressing

In a pressing formation, all players move forward and try to keep the attackers as far away from their own goal as possible. Above all, the player with the ball should not be attacked so long as he/she is positioned far away from the goal. His/her passing stations are always blocked (see Fig. 4.22). Because of the limited possibility of bouncing the ball several times, it is difficult for the player in possession of the ball to approach the goal without passing. At the same time, however, it trains the attacking player to pass and run.

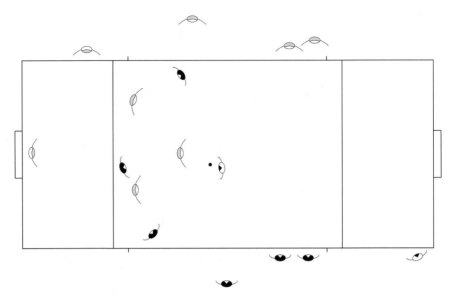

Fig. 4.21 The 2:1 defence formation

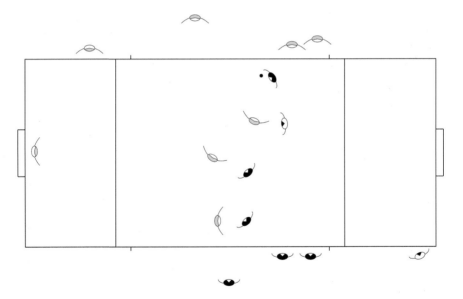

Fig. 4.22 Defence pressing with blocked passing stations

4:0 Offense Formation

In the 4:0 offense formation, the attack-position line is resolved. The attack now takes the positions left wing, centre offense left, centre offense right, and right wing (see Fig. 4.23). The player with the specialist function can be used in different positions here. The positioning has a direct effect on attack and defence behaviour of the team and should be tested variably.

3:1 Offense Formation with a Specialist in a Wing Position

In the 3:1 offense formation, the specialist does not have to play in the centre-offense position. If the specialist is positioned in a wing-position in the 3:1 offense formation (see Fig. 4.24), this changes the attack and defence behaviour of the team significantly. An outside defender will now focus more on the specialist on the side of the field, which will lead to more space for the attack in the central area. However, the player in the offense-centre position is more restricted in his/her actions than the specialist and must therefore create new solutions. The remaining defenders now also have to defend a more open central space.

The Transition Game

The transition game from defensive to offensive is becoming more important, especially with the increased use of substitutes. For the first time, the matching tactical options can now be specifically addressed in the game. The defence of these transition game actions (from offensive to defensive) should not be neglected. However, these can only be trained for implicitly through practice games. The

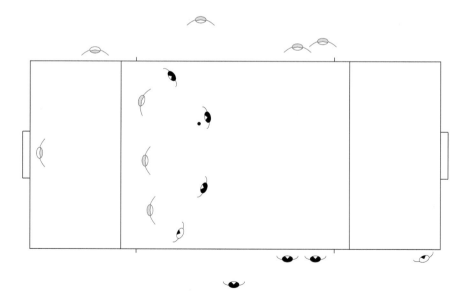

Fig. 4.23 4:0 offense formation with a specialist in a wing position

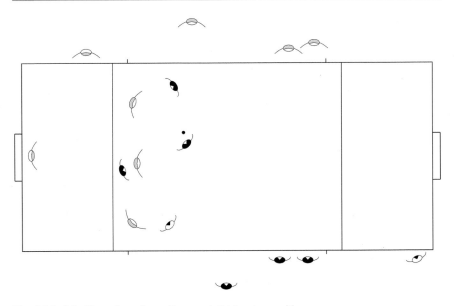

Fig. 4.24 3:1 offense formation with a specialist in wing position

targeted training of this phase of the game is very complex and should only be discussed later in the development process of a beach handball player.

The Task of the Goalkeeper

If a ball is blocked by the goalkeeper, captured by the defence (e.g., by a block), or lands in the goal, the goalkeeper has three options:

1. **The coast-to-coast throw.** The goalkeeper should at all times observe whether the opposing specialist is still on the field after the change of possession. If the change from specialist to the goalkeeper is unsuccessful or takes too long, the goalkeeper can use the situation for a coast-to-coast throw from his/her own goal area at the empty goal (see Fig. 4.25).
2. **The long pass.** If the coast-to-coast throw is not possible or does not make sense, the goalkeeper can use a long pass on his offensive switching players. This long pass is particularly useful and promising if the opposing defensive switching players are not yet on the field or the opponent is taking too long to make their changes (see Fig. 4.26).
3. **The short pass and the possible change for the specialist**. If neither the coast-to-coast throw nor the long pass is possible or useful, the goalkeeper can play a short pass at a runner (see Fig. 4.27). After this pass, the goalkeeper can bring himself/herself in as a specialist in the offensive game or as a substitute for the specialist.

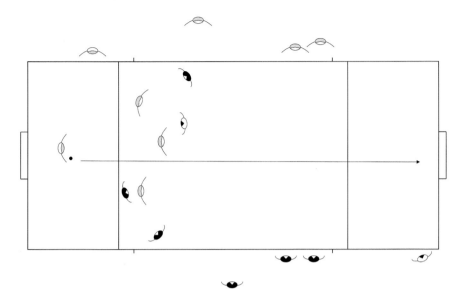

Fig. 4.25 The coast-to-coast throw

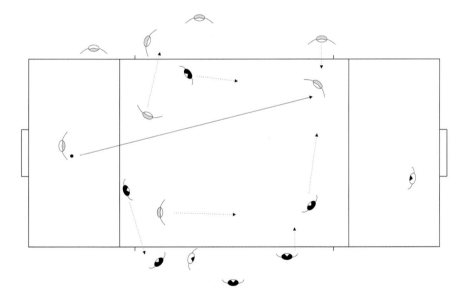

Fig. 4.26 The long pass

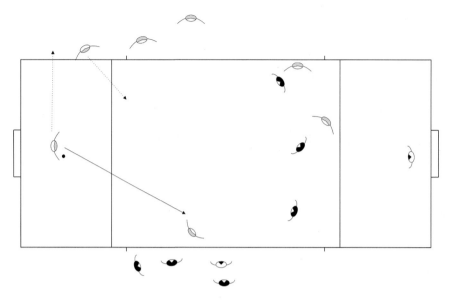

Fig. 4.27 The short pass and the possible change for the specialist

The Task of the Field Players and Specialists

The task of the field players, especially the attacking/defensive players, is to switch from defensive to attacking players when changing possession so quickly that the goalkeeper can use his/her second option, the long pass. If this option is not possible because the opponent has also quickly switched from attacking to defending player, one player should be able to receive the short pass in the runner's position. The short pass and the goalkeeper substituting himself/herself for the specialist does not mean that this play has to be played slowly. Here, too, the switching phase can be used with a quick passing game if the opponent is taking too long to change and switch from offensive to defensive.

> **Less is more**
> The tactical options presented in this chapter can and should be tried out and experienced in training and competition. The athletes should not be overwhelmed; however, a change of formation or a new option should only be introduced if all game activities beforehand have succeeded seamlessly. And please, don't forget, just play! (see Fig. 4.28).

Fig. 4.28 Don't forget: Just play

Further Readings

Deutscher Handballbund (2022) DHB-Rahmentrainingskonzeption Beach Handball. DHB und Münster: Phillipka-Sportverlag, Dortmund
Fasold F, Gehrer A (2020) Beach Handball. From the Grassroots. In EHF scientific conference: fifth EHF scientific conference "Handball for life," documentation (S. 19–23). European Handball Federation

The Basic Tactical and Technical Elements of Beach Handball

5

Contents

Basic Tactics in Beach Handball

The tactical options for action in beach handball are more limited than in indoor handball in one way, because of the reduced number of players, and more variable in another way, because of the additional option in making a scoring decision (does one try to score one point or two?). Some tactical movements in indoor handball can also be found in beach handball, whereas many others can only be found in the beach handball discipline.

(continued)

Supplementary Information The online version contains supplementary material available at [https://doi.org/10.1007/978-3-662-64566-6_5]. The videos can be accessed by scanning the related images with the SN More Media App.

In this chapter, a simple overview of the tactical actions in beach handball is presented. This overview follows the structure of the game phases in Chap. 3, Table 3.1. The tactical actions are divided into individual, cooperative, and collective elements. The special features of the goalkeeper and specialist game are discussed separately in the respective phases of the game.

Game Phase Attack

Collective Actions

Collective actions in attacking play primarily relate to the specifications in which a formation should be played (e.g., 3:1 or 4:0).

The positioning of the specialist has a profound impact on the collective attack game. The position of the specialist always has a direct influence on the actions of the defence, irrespective of the chosen formation.

In addition to the formation, collective actions also dictate how this formation should be played. This play can be adjusted from specifics to a free game with all degrees of freedom in the decisions (where do I play the ball) to each game position, up to a game where the clear 'if-then' rules are manifested. A game with all degrees of freedom is less susceptible to interference by the opposing defence; however, it places high demands on the decision-making ability of all the attackers. A game with clear 'if-then' rules is prone to interference; however, such a game can be easier for players who have difficulty making the right decisions.

In fact, normative requirements such as wanting to play fast or wanting to finish with the spin shot if possible, are seen as collective tactical conditions for playing (see Fig. 5.1).

Cooperative Actions

Cooperative actions relate primarily to the interaction between two attackers (see Fig. 5.2).

Here, elements of the passing game are seen as the basis of all cooperation. The permanent numerical advantage in the attack allows many good opportunities to materialize through a skilful passing game alone. In addition to the passing game in motion, the back pass or double pass game is a simple means of getting players into free goal-throwing situations.

The inflight cooperation is crucial in the passing game. The timing of the pass must be adapted in a way that it corresponds to the start and jump timing of the shooting player.

Simple shifts in the game with the ball to open and expand attack areas on the side, distant from the ball, are also seen as collective actions.

Parallel attack movements take place in almost every attack action, but in beach handball, they can be seen in a further simplified form; that is, an attacker always attacks the open space with the ball parallel to his teammate while anticipating a pass.

Fig. 5.1 Collective play in beach handball (Photo: Alex Gehrer)

Fig. 5.2 Cooperative play in beach handball

Crossing movements or changing positions with and without the ball are also parts of the cooperative game, but these often do not have a direct effect as they do in indoor handball. Instead, they disguise certain actions and formulate others or raise the dynamics in certain game situations to achieve a game advantage.

Screening can also be used for cooperative play, but it can be very dangerous, leading up to a potential offensive foul in beach handball. In individual attacks, indirect screening is mainly used to prepare one's own throw at the goal and, above all, to make space for inflight passes. Direct screening is primarily used when free goal throws by the specialist are possible in the throwing zone next to the goal area line.

Individual Action

The basic individual tactical action, game position or game function regardless, is attacking the goal by approaching and playing in free spaces. Irrespective of the position and function and being in possession of the ball or not, attackers must always act away from the defenders in free spaces in the direction of the goal (see Fig. 5.3).

Game position-specific playing around/overplaying defenders, especially in the wing and centre positions, by quickly changing direction with and without the ball, is the basis for gaining an advantage over the defenders. From the permanent numerical advantage, this is only seen as a subordinate action, rarely with an advantage of 1:1 against a defender.

Fig. 5.3 Individual play in beach handball

Table 5.1 Structural model for tactics of offensive behaviour in beach handball

Collective Actions		
• Attack formation. • Position of the specialist. • Degrees of freedom in actions. • Normative specifications, e.g., "fast game".	Cooperative Actions	
	• Passing game. • Back pass/ double pass. • Inflight pass. • Switch play. • Parallel attack. • Switching positions. • Crossings. • Screens.	Individual Actions
		• Attack goal/open spaces. • Running clear/calling for the ball. • Fakes without ball. • Fakes with ball. • Putting the ball down. • Indirect screening. • Goal throw decision (1 point vs. 2 points).

Because bouncing is irrelevant, putting the ball down must be discussed in connection with the individual tactical game with the ball. On the one hand, this action costs time, but on the other hand, it enables further game actions as three steps are available.

The passing game in general, and the inflight pass in particular, possess a high tactical importance in beach handball as these passes must be played at the optimal time in optimal spaces.

The goal-throwing situation is primarily technical but is subject to the tactical decision-making pressure in the field player position; for example, in deciding whether to use a spin shot for two points or a punch/jump shot for one point.

Depending on the game function, this decision component is not required for the specialist. However, for the specialist, the challenge is to think on a tactical level; on the one hand, on how to influence the greatest goal potential to achieve two points as easily as possible, and on the other hand, to open up the space for the field players so that scoring chances with the maximum possible points arise.

Indirect screens are particularly relevant for field players in the line position, for example, to open a space or keep a space open for an inflight pass.

Table 5.1 represents the interplay between collective, cooperative, and individual game actions in offensive behaviour.

Game Phase Defence

Collective Actions

In the defensive game, collective actions primarily relate to the specifications of which formation should be played (e.g., 3:0, 2:1, pressing). In addition to the formation, the collective action also dictates the choice of such formation. From free defence to clear agreements on where a ball should be gained or a player should be forced to make a throw at the goal, these requirements always apply to the whole team: the collective. This distinction also applies to general guidelines on how and where, for example, blocks should be played.

The permanently outnumbered defence situation means a collective orientation towards the ball is vital. The farthest away and, therefore, the most difficult, pass station for the ball operator is disregarded, and all actions in the vicinity of the ball are focused on collectively.

Cooperative Actions

Cooperative actions relate primarily to the interaction between two defenders, especially between the blockers and the goalkeeper.

Purely related to the field players, the cooperative actions here are decisive in the way that a defender must always react directly to the actions of his/her direct opponent. If a defender steps too far forward, the space also changes for the next defender; therefore, he/she must close this space according to the demands of the situation.

If double blocks are placed or jumped, the two defenders involved must also act optimally with regard to the timing and the space to optimize the likelihood of a successful defensive action.

Cooperation with the Goalkeeper

A block against a throw should always happen in cooperation with the goalkeeper. The blocking player has to agree with the goalkeeper about which corner he/she is blocking. The goalkeeper must fulfil his/her role in the task as agreed upon in such cooperation, covering the other corner of the goal, and identifying whether the field player succeeds in fulfilling his/her task. If this succeeds, the cooperation is clear; if this does not succeed, the goalkeeper must act freely against the throw (see Fig. 5.4).

Individual Actions

The individual basic position of a defender against a direct opponent, as also in indoor handball, only exists against the specialist in beach handball. Here, one should be positioned angularly between the shoulder of the throwing arm and the goal (e.g., against right-handed people, in front of the body on the left side).

A position that is angular to the opponents is recommended against field players. However, this is not based on the throwing arm, and should always steer the opponent into a position that is as unfavourable as possible for their actions (usually towards the side-line).

Stepping out into a pass, or blocking passing pathways and making attempts to open spaces, is fundamental to every individual defensive action. The arms should be positioned in such a way that a passing path can be attacked whenever possible.

Although the upper body remains upright in all actions, hips and knees should be slightly bent because this position makes it easier to quickly react/act in/against the space and change one's direction by moving (forwards, backward, sideways), if need be.

The diver block makes highly technical demands on the defenders. However, this too must be used with due considerations to timing and space. Jump timing should be adapted to the attacker's throwing action so that the optimum range of the block is

Fig. 5.4 Cooperation between defence and goalkeeper in beach handball

achieved when the ball is thrown. The distance to the thrower should be so small that it is as close as possible to the ball, but there is no physical contact.

The Goalkeeper

As part of the individual actions of the goalkeeper, one of the primary objectives is to apply the technical skills (saves) bearing in mind the correct space and the right timing (see Fig. 5.5).

The optimal position is always the one in which the shooter's throwing opportunities are limited to the greatest extent and the area of the goal is optimally covered. The place where the ball leaves the thrower's hand serves as a point of orientation. It is important for a goalkeeper to optimally anticipate this throw-off point to control the outcome.

In terms of the timing, the goalkeeper should come to a steady stance in this position just before the ball is released. From this position, the appropriate action (e.g., a deep save, jump save) to defend the ball can happen.

Although the timing is imperative, the position can be varied with regard to depth (forwards, backward) and width (left, right) in a targeted manner to lure the shooter into a trap (e.g., position which is too far left, throw to the right; position far forward, throw as a toss).

There are other features that are relevant for a goalkeeper from a tactical point of view for defence against spin shots and inflight throws.

Fig. 5.5 Goalkeeper in beach handball

Table 5.2 Structural model for tactics of defensive behaviour in beach handball

Collective Actions		
• Defence formation.	Cooperative Actions	
• Ball orientation.		
• Free vs. agreement.	• Adjust space.	Individual Actions
• Blocking.	• Help out.	
	• Set traps.	• Basic position against opponents.
	• Blocking.	• Basic position against the ball.
	• Cooperation with the goalkeeper.	• Attack passing path.
		• Set traps.
		• Block game.

An attacking player is blind for a brief moment in the spin shot and as he/she turns away from the goal, he/she cannot visually perceive any information about the goalkeeper's action. The goalkeeper can use this blind moment to set traps or pretend to act to force the shooter into a certain throw.

In inflight, the action of the attacking player depends primarily on the moment of his/her flight phase at which he/she can catch the ball. If he/she catches it early, the options for action are open and he/she can watch the goalkeeper and his/her next movements. If he/she catches the ball late during the flight phase, the options for action are limited. The goalkeeper can use this, for example, by acting aggressively, and restrict the throwing options for the shooter.

Table 5.2 represents the interplay between collective, cooperative, and individual game actions in defensive play.

Game Phase Transition: Defence to Offense

Collective Actions

The collective actions in the transition game relate first and foremost to the basic specification of the speed with which the game should be played. A game at high speed puts the opponent under great pressure and facilitates playing out simple goal-throwing opportunities. However, it is associated with a high level of risk and many ball losses. A slow pace brings security and control but also enables the opponent to form a controlled defence.

Relevant for this phase is the change strategy: should the game be played with three, two, one, or even zero runners and three changes?

Furthermore, collective actions refer to the formation in which the tempo game is played: is the formation already being used in transition the same as the one in which the attack will be played later or is another formation selected for the transition phase? Most importantly, the positioning of the specialist has a strong effect on the performance of the opposing defender, even in the transition phase.

Cooperative and Individual Actions

Tactical actions on a cooperative and individual level in the transition phase only differ from those in the attack phase because the time pressure with regard to anticipation, perception, and decisions is significantly heightened. All actions must take place at a higher speed. In the individual area, however, the ball may be put down more often, and larger spaces have to be bridged frequently.

Cooperative and Individual Action of the Goalkeeper from Defence to Offense

The goalkeeper should always consider the first option of the coast-to-coast throw after changing the ball possession. If this is unlikely, the long pass to a substituted attacking player is the second option. If this is also improbable, the goalkeeper must bring the ball into the field with a short pass. Depending on the collective tactical requirements, the goalkeeper can now contribute to the transition game as a specialist (see Table 5.3).

Table 5.3 Cooperative and individual action of the goalkeeper from offense to defence

Cooperative Actions of the Goalkeeper	
• Agreement with the block.	Individual Actions of the Goalkeeper
• Passing game.	• Position and timing against the throw.
• Substitution.	• Set traps.
	• Goal throw.

Game Phase Transition: Offense to Defence

Collective Actions
Collective actions in the transition game to the defence are seen as similar to the game transition to the offense. Switching backwards as quickly as possible prevents simple goals by the opponent and allows the opponent to use a fast and risky game to win the ball.

The change strategy is of particular importance here, as changes must take place as quickly as possible so that the changing players can put the attack under pressure swiftly.

In this context, a changed formation can also be used to counter the attack in the transition game.

Cooperative and Individual Actions
Here, too, all cooperative and individual actions of the defensive game are required at increased speed. However, it would be advantageous to act cooperatively and individually in such a way that the opponent has to put the ball down. Putting a ball down always reduces the speed of the attack.

Cooperative and Individual Action of the Goalkeeper from Offense to Defence
A distinct feature of cooperative play is the changing role of the goalkeeper as the specialist. This change must be done quickly enough so that the goalkeeper enters the field early enough to prevent coast-to-coast attempts by the opponent (see Table 5.3).

Basic Technical Skills in Beach Handball

The movement technique in tasks related to sports is fundamentally defined as the motor procedure that is used to find the best possible solution to a certain sporting movement task. With regard to sport-specific techniques, it is especially about the sport-specific development of the coordination abilities. This chapter describes basic technical skills required at the various phases of beach handball.

Except for the goalkeeper game, the technical skills are described independently of the game positions and game functions here. Among the coordination skills, good movement technique appears to be paramount, primarily because it resolves any given movement task issues. However, the quality of this skill is also reflected in the speed and economy of the movement. Furthermore, a technique is considered to be good if it can be applied and adapted in a targeted manner or safeguarded from disruptive influences.

A technique can rarely be viewed in isolation in any sport, and beach handball is no exception. Tactical components can be found in almost every movement: this is not overlooked in this chapter, but for the sake of simplicity and brevity, technical elements of the game are given more impetus here.

Basic Skills

In beach handball, footwork is seen as a basic technical skill that applies to the offensive, defensive, transition, and also the goalkeeping game. This footwork includes walking, running, or stepping movements in all directions. Footwork also includes jumps and leaps, which are very often used in many game-specific actions, for instance, goal throwing, saves, or blocking situations (see Fig. 5.6).

In addition to basic strength and endurance skills, the ability to maintain an equilibrium while implementing the footwork has an exceptionally large role. The sand, as the subsurface, is challenging to the sense of balance in particular.

Defence

In the defensive game, these basic skills must be combined well to coordinate the leg and arm movements. While the legs are challenged to implement running and jumping movements at the highest intensity, sporadically stable and controlled

Fig. 5.6 Footwork as the basic technical skill for all game phases

Fig. 5.7 Attacking the ball in beach handball

action against the ball, using the arms (blocks, stealing balls etc.) must remain possible (see Fig. 5.7).

Coupling and decoupling of athletes is a challenge during the game, not only on the level of strength skills, but also in the coordination area. Economical, precise, and, therefore, quick movements are an indicator of good movement technique in defensive play.

Diver Block

The specific action of the diver's block against spin shots or other throws is particularly challenging in terms of coordination. In a lateral jump backwards, the arms are brought into a block position against the ball or the path of the ball (see Fig. 5.8). In addition to tactically relevant aspects of the timing and performance in this space, this very specific jump and block technique must be trained. The landing after this block should also be part of the training, as landing sideways from the full length of the body can lead to overload, especially in the neck area. This stress must be offset by training with targeted exercises.

Fig. 5.8 The diver block in beach handball

Execution of the diver block in beach handball. (▶ https://doi.org/10.1007/000-6c4)

Offense

Passing and Catching

In addition to the basic skills mentioned, technical elements primarily include handling the ball. Passing and catching are the basis of all acts of attack. As with

Fig. 5.9 The power position in offense

passing techniques, all throwing techniques can be performed with the appropriate use of force and an appropriate target. The power position must be chosen in the passing game in a way that always enables all passing options. This position is known as the all-options position. Throwing arm postures that limit the pass options (e.g., ball below shoulder height) should generally be avoided. In the power position, the ball is slightly above head height, with the elbow at about shoulder height, with an open body position towards the goal (see Fig. 5.9).

With the catching technique, the aim is to catch the ball with both hands at chest height. The thumb and forefinger of both hands form a reversed heart, while the elbows are bent slightly. Hands and elbows should give in slightly in the direction of the pass when making contact in a suction movement to absorb the energy of the pass. If the pass is played lower than the chest height, the upper body is brought into the correct position by lowering the body. Optimally, catching always takes place in the direction of the opposing goal or the object of the attack (see Fig. 5.10). The ball is received in a small jump in the air to act after three steps.

Throwing

Straight Shot   After catching the ball with a small jump and landing on both legs, a right-hander should put his/her left leg forward for the first step. This step is followed by the step with the right leg, the arm with the ball moving with a swing movement, and the last or third step as a bracing step. In this step, the tip of the braced foot is always pointed in the direction of the target. For stability, the ball is gripped by the fingers during the swing movement and the wrist is opened. The elbow is brought behind the head, a little above shoulder height, and is slightly bent. The ball is, thus,

Fig. 5.10 Catching the ball in offense

slightly above head height (see Fig. 5.9). After the left leg is braced into the ground, the pelvis rotates by moving its right side forward. This movement is followed by a trunk rotation with a simultaneous slight torso flexion. Elbow extension follows immediately after the onset of the shoulder rotation. The ball receives the last impulse by flexing the wrist before the ball leaves the hand.

The movement phases described here (e.g., catching the ball, run-up) are extremely variable in the game (also from the uneven surface) and should, therefore, be trained for with maximum adaptability.

Jump Shot The jump shot is similar to the straight shot in the swing and throwing movements. The last step of the run-up, however, is not carried out as the bracing step, instead, it requires taking off upwards and forwards with the single leg. The other leg is used as a flywheel and the knee is pulled forward and up: the lower leg remains under the body. The execution of the throwing movement is the same here as with the straight shot; that is, the ball leaves the hand during the flight phase of the jump (see Fig. 5.11). Landing after the jump should always be done under the most conscious control possible to avoid instability or injury.

Spin Shot The run-up takes place the same way as previously described for the other options. The ball is received in a slight forward leap on both legs. The spin-shot movement can be initiated from this step or subsequently. To support the rotation of the body, the throwing hand is placed low next to the body and the non-throwing arm in front of the body.

According to the rules, the take-off must be made on both legs with the feet parallel to the middle of the goal (see Fig. 5.12). This way, a 360-degree rotation can

Fig. 5.11 Jump shot in beach handball

Fig. 5.12 Position of feet in the spin-shot take-off

be generated before the goal throw, which is scored with two points if the goal throw is successful.

In the last step before the jump, either both feet are jumped upon (both-legged ground contact), or the second foot is placed next to the first. The feet should be positioned about hip to shoulder width apart. With the knees extended, the throwing arm with the ball is brought in front of the body in the direction of the non-throwing shoulder. The non-throwing arm is moved from the front of the body to the side to the back. Simultaneously, with the movements of the arms, the head is turned in the direction of the rotation (for right-handers to the left, for left-handers to the right).

During the rotational movement, the throwing arm must be moved further upwards. By simultaneously extending the non-throwing arm in the elbow joint, the rotation is slowed down, and the body is opened towards the goal. The release of the ball is similar to the other throws.

Execution of the spin shot in beach handball. (▶ https://doi.org/10.1007/000-6c3)

The execution of the run-up and rotation are shown here as an example. From a technical perspective, the run-up and rotation can vary individually. In the international form of elite beach handball, there are different variations of the execution of the spin shot (e.g., moving the arms upwards at the same time, similar to a turn jump from gymnastics), and these can all be explored. The decisive factor for a successful spin shot is acquiring an individual movement technique in which the fastest possible rotation with the highest possible jump height is generated.

Inflight According to the regulations, inflight goals are rated as successful when the shooter catches the ball in the air after the jump and throws it into the goal before landing. The ball must be caught in a controlled manner before it is thrown (see Fig. 5.13). The inflight always occurs in a cooperative game, and so the pass and the throw actions are described here from a technical perspective.

Passing The passing technique, as explained in 'Passing and Catching,' should be done from the power position in a clear passing movement. Curved passes played

Fig. 5.13 Inflight in beach handball

from this power position, which fall into the hands of the recipient from above, are favourable.

Run-up The thrower should start dynamically achieving the greatest possible jump height. Leaps or steps should not be used, instead, running steps make it easier for the passer to anticipate the passing path. The take-off, especially from the line position, often takes place without a run-up or with just one step. As it is more difficult to achieve a great jump height thus, this has to be trained in a targeted manner. The take-off can be done with one leg or with both legs. The focus here is primarily on the tactical aspects. If one jumps from a standing position, you should jump with both legs for the higher power generation thereof. If the take-off takes place after the run-up, one has the option of jumping on one leg. The arms can be used as a flywheel by explosively moving from the bottom to the top to support the jump height while taking off.

Catching and throwing If the arms are raised when jumping, the ball should be caught at or above head height. The non-throwing hand is released from the ball and by turning the body slightly in the air, the shooter comes directly into an optimal throwing position. The ball can also be caught with one hand. The ball must leave the throwing hand before any part of the thrower's body touches the ground.

Execution of inflight in beach handball. (▶ https://doi.org/10.1007/000-6c2)

Fakes

Fakes in an attack play are defined as all actions with which an attacker creates a spatial and/or temporal advantage over one or more defenders as well as the goalkeeper to successfully complete an attack. In general, many variations of fakes are possible (e.g., visual fakes), but we only describe basic fakes here.

Throwing/passing fakes These fakes are based on the technical features of passing and throwing. After reaching the power position, the passing/throwing movement is initiated, as described for the throwing technique, but is interrupted during the onset of shoulder rotation. To be able to use the ball quickly in another direction or with interrupted timing in the same direction, the shoulder rotation must be carried out only so far that the ball is still at head height. For these fakes to be effective, they should not be carried out too quickly; the defenders must be able to fall for them.

Running fakes with and without the ball Running fakes are changes of direction that are supposed to result in a positional advantage over the defenders. In a normal running movement, after shifting your weight on one leg, the body should be moved swiftly in the other direction. The change of direction should take place with a large, expansive step (see Fig. 5.3); this can be done with or without a ball (with the ball, the 3-step rule must be taken into account).

Technique in the Transition Game

In the transition game from defence to offense, all technical skills of the offensive game are required under the conditions of increased game speed. There are no additional technical requirements, but the increased time and situation pressure makes it even more difficult to perform the attack skilfully.

The same applies to the transition game from offense to defence. Again, no new defence skills are required, but all actions take place at a faster pace.

Goalkeeper Technique

The technical aspects that are mentioned here relate purely to defence against throwing a goal, ball control, and opening the game. The goalkeeping game is characterized by an extremely high degree of individuality, and a wide variety of technical styles and actions can be successful. For this reason, the basis presented here is only intended to be a guideline, and all options for functional expansion remain open.

Defence Against Throws

If the opposing attack is in the build-up phase, the goalkeeper is in his/her basic position. The feet are positioned at about shoulder width, parallel to the ball, and the weight is on the forefoot (heel not in the air). Knees and hips are slightly bent to create tension throughout the body. The arms are bent slightly outwards to the left and right in front of the body at about chest height so that both hands are still in the visual field. In this position, the goalkeeper moves with flat, lateral steps on an arched action line in front of the goal line from post to post.

The basic techniques for defence against a goal relate to the balls thrown at low, mid-high, and high height. With the help of the stride jump technique, which requires jumping from the leg far from the ball, all three goal areas are covered in one corner of the goal.

When the balls are thrown low, the swinging leg should be brought flat over the ground into the corresponding goal corner while using a stride jump. The foot must be brought in the air towards the corner. When the foot is placed on the ground after this action, the tip of the foot points in the direction of the outer line, and the hand near the ball secures an additional area above the foot (see Fig. 5.14).

Alternatively, the foot cannot be put down here, but instead can be moved into the hurdle seat (slide movement) (see Fig. 5.14).

If the ball is thrown high, the goalkeeper should try to get both hands behind the ball to cover as much of the goal area as possible (see Fig. 5.15). However, a save with one hand is also possible and is not a sign of wrong technique.

When the balls are thrown mid-high, in addition to the arms, the swinging leg is pulled up to the middle of the goal to enlarge the areas in the goal that are covered (see Fig. 5.16).

Fig. 5.14 Save of balls thrown low in beach handball

Fig. 5.15 Save of balls thrown high in beach handball

In addition to all the activities in the goalkeeping game, the sandy ground allows significantly more acrobatic or creative jumping actions to defend against goal throwing than the hall floor, as is the case in indoor handball, because the risk of injury on sand is greatly reduced.

If the specialist of his/her own team is attacking, the goalkeeper should always be positioned in the goalkeeper transition area, ready to start, to prevent coast-to-coast throws by the opposing team in the event of a change of possession after substituting for the specialist.

Fig. 5.16 Save of balls thrown mid-high in beach handball

Goalkeeping in beach handball. (▶ https://doi.org/10.1007/000-6c5)

Game Opening

Because beach handball is played without a throw-off after a goal, the opening of the game by coast-to-coast goal throws and the fast pace of a passing game leading to the

Fig. 5.17 Passing on the goalkeeper position in beach handball

concentration of action up front makes the goalkeepers that much more important. On a technical level, jump shots and straight shots can be used here. The straight shot can be executed faster and generates more ball speed, but because of the uneven surface, it is coupled with a significantly higher demand on the goalkeeper's coordination skills (see Fig. 5.17). The jump shot takes a little more time, but the relatively calm jump phase can enable a controlled throw. The goalkeeper's individual technical skills should be considered before deciding which shot can be made. The technical execution of the shots does not differ from those that have been previously described for the field players. The same applies to the goalkeeper's passing game (second and third option); here too, all the technical features of the passing game that have been described for the field players are applicable.

Skill Training and Coaching in Beach Handball Competition

6

Contents

Supplementary Information The online version contains supplementary material available at [https://doi.org/10.1007/978-3-662-64566-6_6]. The videos can be accessed by scanning the related images with the SN More Media App.

Training for Collective, Cooperative, and Individual Actions

The following chapter proposes games and forms of exercise for training specific beach handball skills. Because the contents of this book are primarily aimed at beginners, little consideration is given to the collective game because its basics are laid out in the game forms in Chap. 4. The cooperative game is only discussed in regard to suggestions for the design of exercise and game forms, as this depends on the development of individual skills. To develop individual skills on a technical and tactical level, exercises are shown in detail in line with the game phase model (goalkeeper, attack, defence, transition). It should be noted that the goalkeeper game always runs simultaneously with the other game phases and should, therefore, be integrated into the training of all other contexts. The shoot-out is also advised as a part of organizing the training.

Training for Collective and Cooperative Action

The training for collective action should and must be implemented in game forms and target games, as it always relates to all the players on the field. This book focuses on getting started with beach handball. Sophisticated collective concepts and in-depth training of collective action are only relevant for advanced play. Basic collective content described in Chap. 4 can be improved in target games through simple specifications (e.g., "We play in a 3:0 defence formation").

The cooperative game, however, has a higher relevance for beginners' play. This game can be trained primarily through basic exercises and games.

Basic exercises are forms of exercise that are always based on the spatial conditions of the target game. This basis means that an element of the game is implemented in an exercise, but always in the conditions that are spatially appropriate to the target game (e.g., exercise to improve the pass-back-pass game for spin shot in the wing positions; see Fig. 6.1).

This approach can lead to typical game setups, but condensed by the number of players (e.g., 2 versus 1). In the basic exercises, defenders and attackers can also be given handicaps (e.g., ball in both hands) or additional tasks (e.g., every pass must be played with the weaker hand).

As already stated, basic games are game forms in which the game idea is always implemented (score points, conquer balls) and defence against attack is played. However, these game forms are condensed by the number of players (2 versus 1, 3

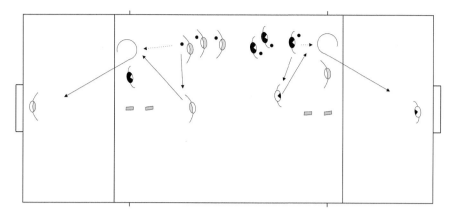

Fig. 6.1 Basic exercise for improving the pass-back-pass game for the spin shot in the wing positions

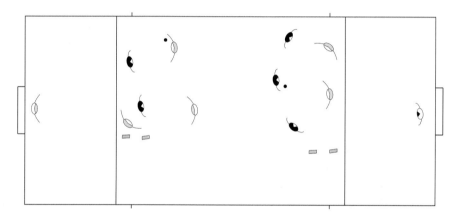

Fig. 6.2 Different line-ups in a basic 3 versus 2 game

versus 2), spatially restricted, or changed. The game functions can also be used variably (with versus without specialist). In these game forms, both attackers and defenders remain free in their actions, but tactical advice can be used to focus on specific game elements (e.g., "We primarily want to get to the goal via inflight"). Figure 6.2 shows two examples of line-ups in a basic 3 versus 2 game. To support the attack game, a passing player can also be positioned next to the play area in basic games.

A competitive character is fundamental for game forms and, thus, also for basic games. There should always be defence against attack in a competition (up to a score, up to several balls wins, on time).

Basic games can be designed very easily and flexibly and, as a result of this as well as the element of competition, are very beneficial for motivation of the athletes.

Based on the training goal, different basic game forms can be easily developed to improve the cooperative game.

Training for Individual Actions

Goalkeeper

In Chap. 3, with the game phase model, it was shown that the goalkeeper game always occurs simultaneously with the other game phases.

Even if the goalkeeper is usually substituted for the specialist in the attacking phase of their team, this does not mean that he/she no longer has a critical task. The duties of the goalkeeper in this phase relate completely to cognitive and psychological areas: the goalkeeper must continue to focus on the new actions and carefully follow the game. This focus must also be trained for; negative experiences must not have any further effects, and a high level of concentration must be maintained over the long term.

In the transition phase from offensive to defensive game, first and foremost, the quick change with the specialist following the rules must succeed and, in the next step, the goal must be occupied as quickly as possible to prevent coast-to-coast throws.

If we look at the transition phase from defensive to offensive, it is the goalkeeper's first option to weigh the throw at the empty goal. If the opposing specialist is still on the field, the throw can be made because the opposing goal is empty. If a substitution of the opponent succeeds, a decision must be made against this option (second option or third option is played).

Throwing and Decision Quality in the Transition Game

The exercise form shown here trains for the transition game and the coast-to-coast action (throwing, changing, throwing defence) of players and goalkeepers alike. There are three attackers in the wing and the centre position, and a goalkeeper in the goal. A goalkeeper crouches on the other side of the field in the goalkeeper changing area.

The three attackers show a free passing game over an arbitrary and variable number of passes. After a few passes, an attacker throws the ball towards the goal with a straight or jump shot. The attacker replaces after the throw as quickly as possible (task of the specialist) so that the other goalkeeper can occupy the empty goal (considering switching rules).

The goalkeeper tries to save the attacker's throw and then to throw the ball coast-to-coast, at the opponent's goal. If the goal is still free, the goalkeeper should definitely attempt this manoeuvre; if the change succeeds, he/she should abort the throw. If the goalkeeper cannot reach the ball after the throw, he/she can take a ball lying next to the goal and attempt to throw coast-to-coast.

At this time, the substitute goalkeeper must observe very carefully when he/she is allowed to enter the playing field (only when the throwing attacker is out) and

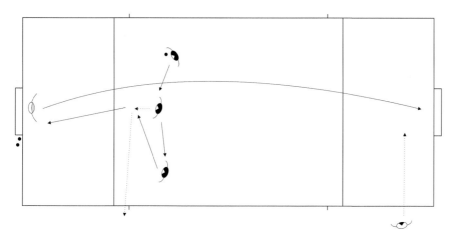

Fig. 6.3 Exercise form to improve the transition game and the coast-to-coast action (throwing, changing, throwing defence) of goalkeepers

occupy the goal in a sprint. If necessary, he/she has to fend off the coast-to-coast throw from the other side with a dive (see Fig. 6.3).

The aim of this action is to train for the coast-to-coast throw and the perception of the game situation (should I throw?). To train for the coast-to-coast throw technically, throwing tasks can be given (e.g., only jump throws, throws with the wrong leg in front), or you can work with changed materials or ball size (smaller versus larger balls).

Throwing and Decision Quality in the Transition Phase with the Second Option

The structure of the exercise here is identical to the one already elaborated. However, the game is expanded to include a defender against the three attackers and one offensive and one defensive switching player. The execution is the same as in the previous exercise, but now the defender and another attacker leave the field after the throw, and a different attacker and a different defender change on the other side (see Fig. 6.4).

For the defending goalkeeper, the first option of the coast-to-coast throw is still available. If this option does not seem feasible, the goalkeeper should play the second option, passing to the alternating attacker. If this is also is not possible, he/she can cancel the action.

For the defending goalkeeper, it is important to switch in time and prevent the coast-to-coast throw. If the second option is played, the goalkeeper tries to fend off the attacker's action together with the defender.

The objective and focus of the observations here are identical to the first form of exercise but are expanded to include the additional decision-making component (second option).

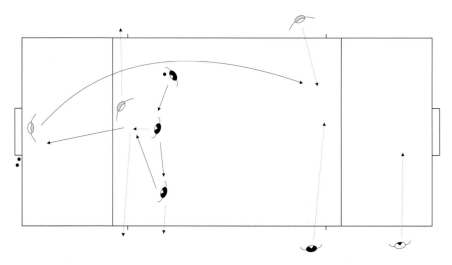

Fig. 6.4 Extended exercise form to improve the transition game and the coast-to-coast action (throwing, changing, throwing defence) of goalkeepers

The Defence of Goal Throws/the Saves

Integrated Goalkeeper Training

The basic technical and tactical components for defending the ball are described in Chap. 5. In the following section, however, no exercise forms are described; instead, the basic principles and possibilities of integrated goalkeeper training are outlined. Goalkeeper skills are trained for in exercise forms for the skills required as a field player.

This integrated goalkeeper training is intended to comply with the game phase model (Chap. 4), which is also reflected in the training content. If the field players train for a certain skill (e.g., the diver block), the goalkeepers can also train for a certain skill simultaneously (e.g., positioning against spin shots).

Most of the exercises for training for field player skills presented in this chapter end with goal throws. The goalkeepers should not simply save these goal throws but also be trained with additional tasks. The goalkeepers are only free from tasks in their game when it comes to free forms of play.

For the integrated and thus simultaneous goalkeeper training, different principles can be considered and applied.

> **The principle of simplification through throwing instructions**
> The field players are instructed within an exercise form to throw only into certain areas of the goal (e.g., only flat). The goalkeepers know this and can, therefore, fully concentrate on the execution of the appropriate saves and actions.

The principle of aggravation by additional tasks
The goalkeepers are given an additional task before the parades (e.g., skipping, handling two extra balls) (see Fig. 6.5). From this additional task, they must proceed to their actions and are thus once again challenged.

The principle of optimization through variation of movements
The goalkeepers have to perform their actions in different variations (e.g., large versus small movements, fast versus slow movements). These variations of a certain action should challenge and support, in particular, the individual optimal actions.

The principle of changing the basic position
The goalkeepers are free to defend the balls, but they have to do it from very offensive (on 2–2.5 m) or very defensive (on the goal line) positions. Their choice of action is thus changed, and their perception is challenged and trained for in particular.

Fig. 6.5 Integrated goalkeeper training with additional tasks

The principle of reaction, action, and deception
Goalkeepers act freely in their game and must either perform their actions very late, as a pure reaction, or very early, as a planned action (e.g., speculating on a corner). A third variant would be the game with deceptions: in each action, the goalkeeper should be offered a corner or a certain throw by the choice of positioning and actions.

The principle of free play in the game
If the field players are allowed to play freely (in both a basic game and a target game), the goalkeepers should also be allowed to play freely.

These principles can be used not only individually but also be combined as required. It is only important that the content is concentrated on individual elements. Because it is not always possible to focus on everything, the goalkeeping skills should be developed step by step.

Separated Goalkeeper Training
In addition to the integrated goalkeeper training just described, goalkeeper actions can of course also be trained separately: a coach works with the goalkeepers in exercises separate from the training of the field players (see Fig. 6.6). The goalkeeper can also be supported by field players for realization of the goal throws.

Such a training form is particularly suitable in the phases of new learning or for working on very specific error patterns or the corresponding potentials. A specific skill (e.g., defence against high balls) should be trained with many repetitions. When designing such exercise sessions, it is recommended that the following principles be observed.

The principle of throwing from realistic distances
Specific movements should always be made against throws from realistic distances. These distances can also be varied selectively to simplify the throw or make it more difficult. However, if, for example, the defence of throws from the spin shot is trained for, the throws should also be made from the appropriate distance.

Fig. 6.6 Separated goalkeeper training in beach handball

The principle of tempo control
Performing movements in slow motion or at an exaggerated speed improves the idea of movement, on the one hand, and makes it easier to find one's own optimal movement tempo, on the other.

The principle of autogenous training
Training for the goalkeeper actions may take place selectively in this separate method, even without balls being thrown at the goal. The actions in "Pantomime" should always be performed with a strong focus on the goalkeepers' imagination: they have to imagine an imaginary ball which they then have to defend.

The principle of acyclic and unique actions

Goalkeeper movements are acyclic and unique. From a variable position, a goalkeeper must perform the fastest and most precise movement, after which this action is finished. Traditionally known throwing series, in which the goalkeepers rhythmically perform actions one after the other, can be justified for warm-up phases in a training session but are not suitable in the larger training content.

The principle of quality over quantity

Even if high repetition numbers are a part of the aim of such separated goalkeeper sessions, an exercise form should be terminated when movement quality suffers.

The principle of balanced success/failure

The degree of difficulty of the reactions to the goal throws should be chosen so that at least every second ball can be successfully saved. To positively set actions in the brain, success is important. Failures on a manageable scale also have a high priority here; they keep the campaigns exciting and motivate the athlete to improve.

Field Player/Specialist in Attack

In the following section, practice and game forms for field players (specialist) for training for basic attacking skills are described (see Fig. 6.7).

Passing and Catching on the Attacking Positions

Three attackers each stand at the left wing, centre offense, and right wing positions. Two defenders, with jerseys in their hands, stand against them (see Fig. 6.8).

The task of the attackers is to pass the ball across the positions. The ball should always be received with a small jump and a forward movement. After the ball is received, it should be passed from the power position.

Fig. 6.7 Training for field players/specialists

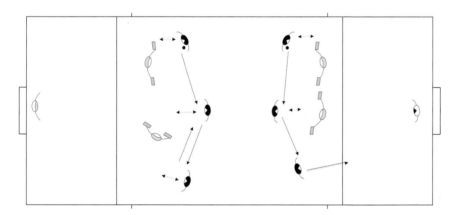

Fig. 6.8 Exercise form to carry out pass and catch actions in typical game positions under variable pressure conditions by the defenders

The defenders block the passing paths from time to time, put the attackers under pressure with the jerseys, and make the passing game more difficult but allow it. After five to eight passes there is an acoustic signal from one of the defenders ("hop"); at this moment, the attacker in possession of the ball is allowed to take a goal throw of his choice (jump shot, straight shot, spin shot). After the throw, both attacking and defending positions are changed.

The aim is to carry out pass and catch actions in typical game positions with variable pressure tactics by the defenders.

The main points of the coaches' observations should be the ball reception in the forward movement, catching the ball with a slight jump, and leading the throwing arm into the power position. Furthermore, it is important that after a pass has been played, a backward movement takes place immediately and the next ball can be caught again in a forward movement.

Passing and Catching in Transition

The goalkeeper plays a long pass (1) to a player running into the field from the substitution area. This player plays a double pass (2 and 3) with another player running into the field. After the double pass, he/she passes to the other goalkeeper (4). Both players leave the field immediately after this pass. Once they have left the field, the goalkeeper plays a long pass (5) to the substitute players on the other side (see Fig. 6.9).

They now perform the same sequence (double pass, pass to goalkeeper, substitution), and the ball is passed to the other side again (pass 1).

The exercise is to be carried out as a continuum, but it should be remembered that the positions are changed in between events.

The aim here is the training for passing and catching over longer distances and under difficult conditions through continuous substitution.

Here, too, the focus of observation is on catching the ball in an easy jump and passing from the power position. Moreover, substituting in and out (albeit under

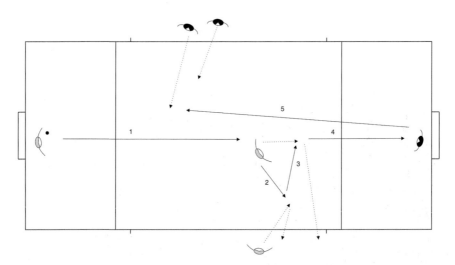

Fig. 6.9 Continuum to train for passing and catching over longer distances and under difficult conditions through substitution

nonspecific conditions) can be trained. No player is allowed to enter the field until a player on the other side has left the field.

Straight Shot and Jump Shot

The variants, straight shot and jump shot, to finish the exercise with a goal attempt are mainly relevant for attackers in the role of specialist. However, these throwing techniques will be needed to score 1-point goals in all other playing positions as well, and these techniques also improve passing skills.

In the sense of a variable training of these techniques, this chapter does not explicitly discuss a run-up rhythm and a lead pattern technique. Instead, forms of exercise are suggested under which an individually optimal technique should develop while observing certain nodes.

The "Waiter" Analogy for Training the Straight and Jump Shot

Straight shot (see Fig. 6.11, left side) Attackers stand with the ball between two markers at a distance of about 4 m from the goal area line. From there, a double pass is played while standing with a passing player in the middle. After the ball has been caught in the standing position, it is passed from the power position. The athlete is now told the following analogy: "You are a waiter, and the ball is a tray on which glasses are placed. Hold the tray in such a way that none of the glasses falls. Then

Fig. 6.10 The "waiter" analogy for training of straight and jump shot

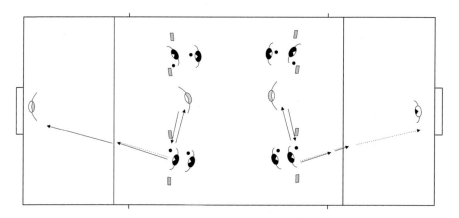

Fig. 6.11 Straight shot exercise (left side) and jump shot exercise (right side)

you run and throw the tray with the glasses into the goal at the goal area line" (see Fig. 6.10).

The distance of the markers to the goal area line must be adjusted so that the athletes do not take more than three steps during the action.

Jump shot (see Fig. 6.11, right side) The task and structure are identical to the straight shot exercise. However, the analogy instruction is changed in the following form: "You are a waiter, and the ball is a tray on which glasses are placed. Hold the tray so that none of the glasses falls down. Then you run and jump over the goal line and throw the tray with the glasses into the goal before you land."

This exercise aims to introduce the jumping and straight shot techniques. The waiter analogy allows the athletes to implicitly assume the correct throwing position (throwing arm raised, left shoulder in front for right-handers, right shoulder in front for left-handers) and in the last step, take a bracing step (straight shot) or jump off with the leg diagonal to the throwing hand (right-handers' left leg, left-handers' right leg). For the exercise form to work, each athlete must have a ball that he/she can grip well and safely. Methodic balls (smaller sizes, soft balls) can also be used for this purpose.

Here, the observation focuses on the throwing arm position (elbow at about shoulder height), the alignment to the goal (non-throwing arm shoulder in the front), and the bracing step or take-off. The waiter analogy used works well implicitly for the most part, and if problems arise, they can be resolved with explicit instructions (e.g., "jump off with your left leg").

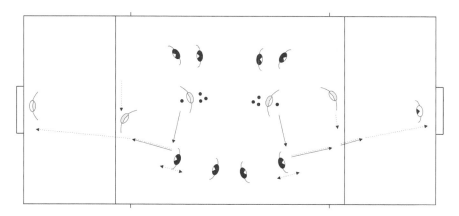

Fig. 6.12 Run-up and variable finish in straight (left side) and jump shot (right side)

Run-Up and Variable Finish in Straight and Jump Shots

The attackers stand without the ball to the left and right of a passing player (see Fig. 6.12). The passing player has all the balls. An attacker runs forward–backward with swift footwork, and at some point receives a pass from the passing player. This pass is to be received in the forward movement, and the ball is then thrown at the goal with a straight shot or a jump shot.

There is a defender in the centre defence position. After the pass, this defender runs into the attacker's space in such a way that the attacker can only finish by passing him/her with a quick straight shot (Fig. 6.12, left side). Alternatively, the defender leaves the attacker a lot of space, which the attacker should use with a jump shot to the goal area (Fig. 6.12, right side). The defender may jump a diver block against this jump shot.

The aim here is to train for ball reception under variable conditions and the direct conversion of this ball into a straight shot or jump shot situation. Furthermore, it should be decided spontaneously under situational pressure whether to take a jump shot or a straight shot.

The focus of observation here is the run-up (no bouncing, only running movements), throwing arm posture, and the decision of whether to use a jump shot or a straight shot. All other observation points are identical to the first exercise form and must also be corrected here or supported with positive feedback.

Spin Shot: Introduction

Several attackers stand with a ball near the goal area line, on the left side with a distance of 1 m and on the right side with a distance of 2 to 3 m (see Fig. 6.13).

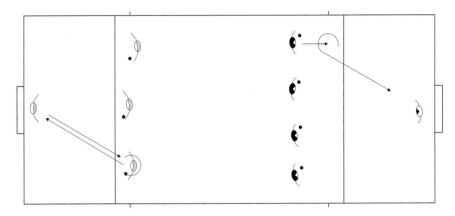

Fig. 6.13 Exercise for introducing the spin-shot technique with a focus on perceptual skills in rotation (left side) and take-off (right side)

On the left side of the field, the athletes perform a rotational jump one after the other with a safe landing on both legs facing the goal. When they have landed, they play a double pass with the goalkeeper. The extent of the rotation must be adjusted at the beginning to ensure a safe landing facing the goal. This extent is then to be increased bit by bit until a 360-degree rotation is achieved. The rotations (in both directions) are to be performed by all athletes once with the left arm as the throwing arm and once with the right arm as the throwing arm.

On the right side, the athletes make a run-up from one or two steps, then jump in on both legs for the take-off. From this jump, they attempt a spin shot towards the goal. The amount of rotation here should also be approached in small steps to a 360-degree rotation in the air.

The aim here is to introduce the spin-shot technique with a focus on perceptual skills in rotation (left side) and take-off (right side). Training for bi-directional rotation is not intended to change the throwing arm dominance, but is helpful in the learning process of the movement, regardless of handedness.

The focus of observation here is on the supporting movements of the arm (in the direction of rotation) and the take-off to the spin shot. A progressive increase in the extent of the rotation is important; the 360-degree rotation does not have to be achieved immediately.

Improvement of Take-Off and Throwing Arm Position in the Spin Shot

Variation A (see Fig. 6.14, left side): There are attackers on the wing positions and a passing player with balls on the centre offense position. The attackers make two-legged jumps over markers or small hurdles in front of them. They variably

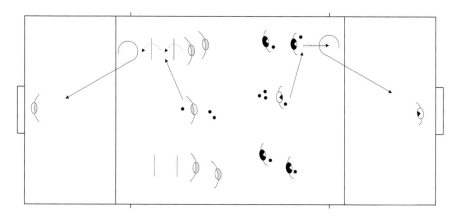

Fig. 6.14 Exercise for improving the take-off and throwing arm position in the spin shot (variation A, left side; variation B, right side)

receive a pass from the passing player (sometimes before the first jump, sometimes after the last) and go into a spin shot when all the hurdles have been jumped over.

Variation B (see Fig. 6.14, right side): The formation is the same here as in variation A, but each attacker has an additional ball in his hand. After a pass from the passing player, the attackers must perform a spin shot to the goal after a variable run-up (one, two, or three steps), but they have the second ball in the non-throwing hand the whole time and do not throw it to the goal.

The aim here is to improve the take-off, the guidance of the throwing arm, and body stability in the movement (run-up, rotation, and throw).

The focus of observation is on the take-off and the guidance of the throwing arm in the rotation. Variation B ensures that the second hand cannot be used to secure the ball during the rotation. It is important to use a ball material that the athletes can grip well. Soft methodic balls can also be used for this purpose.

Inflight: Introduction

A defender and a line player stand in a marked central play area. The defender is holding a ball with both hands. With the ball, a specialist stands at the centre offense position and plays a double pass with a passing player on the side (see Fig. 6.15). The specialist either takes the shot or plays an inflight pass to the line player. If neither appear feasible, he/she may continue to play pass with the passing player.

The defender either clearly confronts the specialist to prevent the throw (see Fig. 6.15, right side) or stays defensively with the line player to make the inflight pass more difficult (see Fig. 6.15, right side). The specialist makes his/her decision (throw versus pass) dependent on the reaction of the defender. The defender should

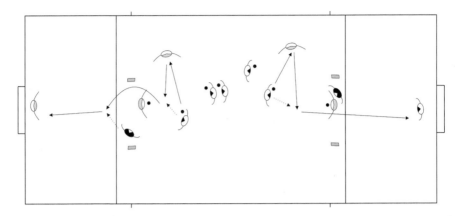

Fig. 6.15 Exercise for introducing the inflight with variations in the defensive play (left side, the defender clearly confronts the specialist; right side, the defender stays defensively with the line player)

Fig. 6.16 The power position to shoot at the goal or play a pass

make it clear early on if he/she is going to step out or stay behind to make it easier for the attacker. Also, the defender may fake his/her intention.

The aim here is to improve the decision-making behaviour on whether to play an inflight pass in the role of the specialist or to throw at the goal. The inflight pass should be played with a steep trajectory so that it falls from the top to the bottom into the hands of the jumping line player. The line player should catch the ball in the jump about 1 m behind the goal area line.

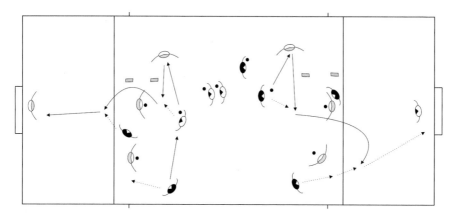

Fig. 6.17 Exercise for improving inflight passes also over long distances

The focus of observation is the decision-making behaviour, especially the specialist's throwing arm position in the passing game (power position) (see Fig. 6.16). Also, the trajectory of the ball (steep ball falling from top to bottom) should be a focus.

Inflight Over Longer Distances

Without one of the two wing positions (delimited by a marker), three attackers play against two defenders. The defenders each hold a ball in both hands. The attackers have a passing player whom they can use (see Fig. 6.17).

On the left side, the attackers play with a specialist but are only allowed to score points via inflight or jump and straight shots. On the right side, the same is played without a specialist, but the attackers may also use spin shots.

The aim here is to also improve inflight passes over longer distances (to the wing positions, from the wing positions) in a relatively free basic game. The different tasks (with a specialist without a spin shot, without a specialist with a spin shot) should additionally train the decision-making behaviour.

As in the first exercise, the focus of observation is the decision-making behaviour, but most importantly, the throwing arm position and the inflight passing game are analysed. In addition, the wing players, in particular, must now be in a permanent state of readiness for a run-up to the inflight, which must also be a focus.

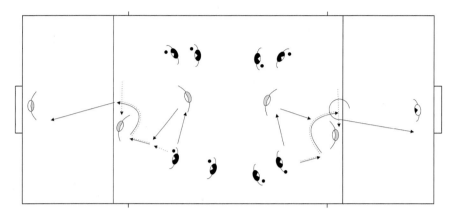

Fig. 6.18 Running fakes with (left side) and without (right side) the ball

Fakes

Running Fakes with and Without the Ball

Variation A: The attackers stand with the ball to the left and right to a passing player (see Fig. 6.18). One defender stands as centre defence at the height of the far goal post. When the attacker passes the ball to the passing player, the defender may run to get an optimal position against the attacker. Here, the defender serves only as an optical aid, and must, even with the knowledge that the attacker changes his/her direction, run for the position close to the goal.

After the pass, the attacker runs straight towards the goal and makes a swift change of direction to the side against the direction of the defender. He/she gets the ball from the attacker either before he/she changes direction (fake with the ball, Fig. 6.18, left), or after he/she has changed direction (fake without the ball, Fig. 6.18, right). The goal finish is free and can be executed as a jump shot, a straight shot, or a spin shot.

Variation B: The same procedure remains as in variation A, except that the attacker receives the ball each time before the change of direction. If the defender is too slow, he/she goes straight into a scoring action without changing direction. If the defender manages to get into position, he/she has to work with a fake with the ball to get an advantage again.

The aim here is to improve changes of direction and thus, deceptive actions, with and without the ball. In variation B, an additional decision component is added (fake or no fake).

The focus of observation is the run-up and the speed of the change of direction. The run-up can be performed at a moderate pace, but the change of direction must be performed at maximum speed. Another point to focus on is the reception of the ball, which should take place shortly before the change of direction to allow taking three more steps.

Training of Further Fakes

Straight shot/pass fakes especially have a very high value also and are an effective attacking tool in beach handball. Passing and running fakes can also be combined in cooperative play. No separate exercise or game forms are offered here for training for these fakes; rather, they should be a component of all exercise and training forms.

Field Player Defence

The following section presents practice and game forms for field players to train for basic defensive skills.

Training for Footwork

Two athletes face each other in front of a line; each holds a ball in both hands, and they try to hold a third ball in the air with this ball (see Fig. 6.19). The ball to be played may be touched several times with the ball in the hands; both hands must always remain on the ball.

The athletes play together and try to keep the ball in the air as much as possible (see Fig. 6.20, left side).

Athletes must use their legs for running, stepping. and jumping movements to get into an optimal position to play the ball.

The exercise can also be done with more than two players, in which case the line should be broken up and the ball played freely. A player who has played the ball

Fig. 6.19 Bounce ball to improve footwork

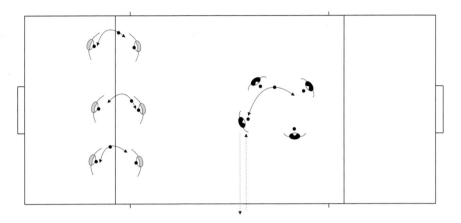

Fig. 6.20 The game bounce ball with two (left side) or more than two (right side) players

must thereafter cross a field line or another marker and may re-enter the game (see Fig. 6.20, right side).

The aim here is to perform running movements under coordinative demanding conditions; orientation, balance, and coupling skills are required. The athlete's visual system is simultaneously challenged as the ball must always be kept in sight.

The observation focus is on clean and intense footwork.

Training of Footwork Through Running with Double Passes and Throwing

One athlete stands in the goal area or about 5 m away from a line. He/she plays continuous double passes with another athlete standing behind the line (see Fig. 6.21). The standing player gives movement instructions ("left," "right," "forward," "backward"). If he/she does not play a double pass but instead throws the ball

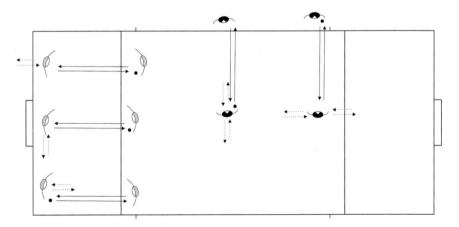

Fig. 6.21 Training of footwork through running with double passes and throwing

in the air, the running player makes a stretch jump and gets a last pass. After that, the tasks are switched.

As before, the aim here is to perform running movements under demanding coordinative conditions; orientation, balance, and coupling skills are also required. The additional task of the passing game simultaneously directs the visual system specific to the game and brings the focus of the athlete away from the footwork alone.

Here, too, the focus of observation is on clean and intensive footwork. At the same time, passing and catching at distances close to the game are trained for here.

Block Against Jumping and Straight Shots

One attacker stands in the central attack position facing the other goal. One defender stands on the central defender position (see Fig. 6.22). After a pass to a passing player, the attacker runs around a centrally placed marker (e.g., a jersey in the sand, a cone) and turns towards the goal. After receiving the ball, he/she finishes either with a jump shot or a straight shot from the playing field (no jumping into the goal area). The passing player has to vary the timing of the pass (early versus late) so that the attacker gets into different throwing situations. The attacker must observe the step rule in his/her action and may not put the ball down.

The defender must touch one of the side markers after the attacker's pass and then try to block the jump or straight shot (see Fig. 6.23). The defender and attacker exchange the task after three actions.

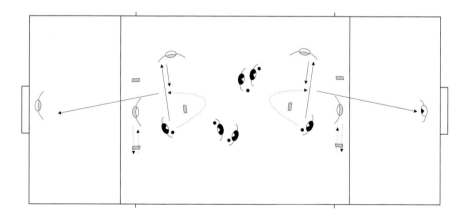

Fig. 6.22 Exercise for improving the blocking game against throws from a specialist from a long distance

The aim here is the variable improvement of the blocking game against throws from a specialist from a long distance.

Fig. 6.23 Blocking against shots from a long distance

The focus of observation here should be on footwork, the position against the thrower (aligned with the throwing arm), distance to the thrower (approximately 1.5 m), and, if necessary, timing in the jump to the block. Another focus should be on the position of the arms in the block situation and the eye behaviour of the athlete (eyes open and throwing arm in view).

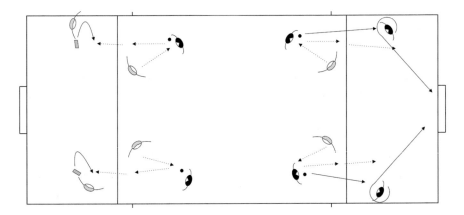

Fig. 6.24 Introducing the diver block by catching a jersey with both hands (variation A, left side) or by blocking a throw (variation B, right side)

Fig. 6.25 Catching a shirt as a start to learn the diver block

Diver Block: Introduction

Variation A (see Fig. 6.24, left side): Two players stand in the corners of the goal area about 2 to 2.5 m from the goal area line and have a jersey in their hands. Two defenders stand at the defence left and defence right positions, and two attackers with the ball stand at the wing positions.

The defenders run as fast as possible to the attackers with the ball and touch the ball. When the ball is touched, the player in the goal area throws the jersey into the air. After touching the ball, the defenders run as fast as possible to the goal area line, jump, and try to catch the jersey with both hands (see Fig. 6.25).

After that, the tasks of the three athletes involved are alternated.

Variation B (see Fig. 6.25, right side): Two players stand in the corners of the goal area about 2 to 2.5 m from the goal area line. Two defenders stand on the defence left and defence right positions, and two attackers with the ball on the wing positions. The defenders run at maximum speed to the attackers with the ball and touch this ball. When the ball is touched, the attacker passes the ball to the player in the goal area. He/she catches the ball and, without changing position, makes a pirouette (without a jump, no spin shot) in the sand, and from this throws the ball at the goal. After touching the ball, the defenders run as fast as possible to the goal area line, jump, and try to block the throw from the pirouette (see Fig. 6.26).

The aim here is to introduce the diver block in terms of the jump, stretching the arms in the air, and the block position against the ball. Because landing with stretched arms causes high stress for the back and neck muscles, this can be particularly focused on in variation A.

Fig. 6.26 Blocking easy throws as the next step in learning the diver block

The focus of observation here should be on the jump (distance to the goal area line), stretching of the arms (in the jump), and alignment against the ball. Focus on the landing and the body tension during the landing should also be maintained at all times.

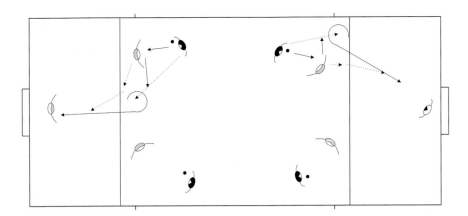

Fig. 6.27 Improving the timing of the jump for the diver block and the distance to the attacker from different positions

Distance and Timing in the Diver Block

A defender and an attacker face each other on the wing positions. The goals are manned by goalkeepers (see Fig. 6.27).

The attacker passes the ball to the defender. The defender blocks, hits, or dredges the ball variably into the sand within a radius of approximately 4 m. The attacker picks up this ball and goes for a spin shot at the goal while observing the step rule (putting the ball down is allowed).

The defender clearly opens a space for the attacker to make his/her spin shot. The defender tries to defend this spin shot with a diver block.

The aim here is to train for the timing of the jump for the diver block (jump attacker before jump defender) and the distance to the attacker. The distance should be chosen so that the defender is as close as possible to the attacker but does not touch him/her.

The observational focus is on the timing and feedback here (earlier, later). The distance to the attacker should be somewhat greater at the beginning (there is a risk of collision during the first attempts) and then gradually reduced. The distance to the line at the jump and also the footwork to the jump should be a further focus.

Shoot-Out Skill Training

All technical and also tactical elements that are described for the successful completion of the shot or the successful defence of a shoot-out action are trained for in the suggested exercise and game forms.

Because the shoot-out poses special challenges to the athletes, especially from a psychological perspective, it is advisable to focus on this in training forms as well.

This action is achieved mainly through a permanent integration of competitions. Further modifications can also make the task easier (e.g., two attackers run to the shoot-out and are still allowed to play a pass) or more difficult (e.g., the ball may only be caught one-handed). Loud music, a wet ball, shoot-out actions against the low sun, etc. can be introduced in this situation to simulate stress in the shoot-out actions.

Shoot-out skills training should be part of every training session because of the importance of the shoot-out.

Video Feedback Training

In the learning process of movements and actions in the sport of beach handball, it is not always easy to visualize your own self in play and implement the corrections made by the coach. A simple method to support this learning process is visual feedback via video recording. What a few years ago was still associated with a high level of technical effort can now be implemented relatively easily in beach handball training, in sports lessons, or training sessions with the use of high-end technology. Smartphones or tablet PCs combined with sometimes inexpensive applications now offer the simplest options for video feedback.

Basics
The use of video analysis and video feedback training should be well thought out so that it does not interfere in the training as a technical gimmick and is instead effective in learning.

Various approaches can be pursued in video training. Although video instructions are reduced to the presentation of models, observable video training can be carried out as a review of a training session or a competition. Video feedback, in turn, relates to immediate feedback following a movement or action with the direct possibility of repeating this action.

Implementation in Practice
The overarching goals of training sessions are mostly beach handball-specific motor and cognitive-tactical learning processes. Video feedback training can accelerate and optimize these processes and make them more effective. Because the video image requires a conscious examination of one's movement/action, video feedback training should be assigned to the explicit learning processes more commonly. Video feedback with the spoken instruction of the coach can and should be supported and controlled.

To design video feedback training effectively, planning must include the perspective of the video image, the concrete content of the video image, the frequency of the feedback, and the timing of the feedback.

Perspective
The camera perspective should be chosen in such a way that the learner has to engage in as little mental rotation effort as possible. Therefore, it is advisable to film the learner from behind, as he/she can 'enter' the video image without mental rotation. However, if a movement or action feature relevant to the selected exercise is hidden, another perspective must be selected. The perspective of the video should, therefore, always be chosen bearing in mind the perfect balance between beach handball elements and the least possible mental rotation effort.

From Global to Detailed Control
A global observation for the learner should only be given at the beginning. After initial experience (one or two repetitions), the focus should be directed relatively quickly to individual relevant movement/action features (e.g., rotation in the jump, timing in the run-up).

Express Content in an Action-Oriented Manner
In terms of content, factual negative feedback (e.g., "That was nothing. Look at your elbow, it's too low again.") can lead to short-term error corrections but has proven to be more of a disadvantage for internalization process of the feedback. Action-oriented positive feedback (e.g., "Better! But try to take your elbow a little higher") seems to be more advantageous in terms of the sustainability of the learning process.

From Much to a Little Feedback
As with verbal feedback, frequent feedback (up to 100%) should be given in new learning phases because this reduces errors in the short term. Usually, this can be reduced significantly after two to three repetitions, and it is sufficient to only support every third or fourth action with video feedback. This reduced feedback is shown to be more effective, especially concerning the sustainability of learning processes.

Video Feedback at the Right Time
The time between the movements should take place at certain intervals. Immediately after the execution, a short period is appropriate for the trainee to process (at least 5 s). However, the video feedback should take place promptly (maximum, 25 s), otherwise the learner will start forgetting the action. After the video feedback, some time (5 s) is recommended for the learner to process it. The renewed movement execution with the integrated feedback should then take place a maximum of 120 s after the feedback.

Required Material
Smartphones can be used in the same way as tablet PCs, but the latter offer better options for optimal use of the visual feedback with the larger screen. The chosen device must have a camera that records enough images (30 fps or more). Inexpensive devices on the market already meet this requirement. There are also various applications for generating video feedback, mostly for less than 10 €. These apps, however, should have the possibility to regulate the video delay. The user should be able to choose the time delay with which the recorded video image is played back. A split-screen function can also be advantageous, in which, for example, the screen is quartered, and the video is displayed with a different delay on each of the screens. For instance, the learner can look at his/her action four times in a row, for example, after 7, 12, 17, and 22 s.

Only a tripod (with a bracket) and a tablet with an installed video app are required as material.

Because strong sunshine makes the picture difficult to see, or light rain can damage the device, it is recommended to attach a small umbrella to the tripod.

Practical Implementation

Based on the points just listed, a design of the exercise repetitions with corresponding instructions is proposed here using the example of the diver block. These repetitions of the action must be integrated into the right time context in an organizational structure of the training session.

1. Repetition: Enable the learner to have a global view: "Look at yourself. What do you see? Can you think of what?"
2. Repetition: Provide a detailed view for the learner: "Make sure that you move more strongly towards the block with your left arm."
3. Repetition: Check details: "And? Which arm did you use?"
4. Repetition: Without video feedback.
5. Repetition: Without video feedback.
6. Repetition: Check details: "How does it look? Good, but you can see that you can bring your left arm further towards the ball.".
7. Repetition: Without video feedback.
8. Repetition: Without video feedback.

In the following segment, an example of the organization for a training group (approximately 10 athletes) with the use of video feedback is explained.

Topic: Improving Arm Posture in the Diver Block

To be able to implement a diver block effectively and successfully, the posture and position of the arms in addition to the jump are relevant. This ability should be trained in the form of exercise and supported with video feedback.

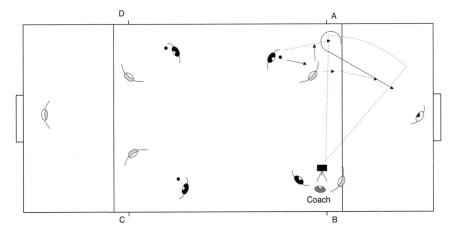

Fig. 6.28 Camera perspective for recognizing and correcting the position of the arms without mental rotation effort

Structure and process At the beginning of the exercise, the posture of the arms in the diver block should be discussed to create an initial idea for the athletes. After the action areas have been determined (see Fig. 6.28, positions A–D), each of these is occupied by an attacker and a defender.

The attacker has a ball and passes it to the defender. The defender throws the ball in the sand in front of him/her. The attacker picks up this ball and takes a shot at the goal (spin shot or jump shot). The defender jumps a diver block against the throw.

In position A, the attackers and defenders run immediately after the action (10 s) to position B and look at the tablet/video feedback system. Here the defender receives feedback via video that is supported with instructions from the coach. The attacker should also observe and analyse the action to learn indirectly from it. Immediately afterwards, the defender tries to implement the feedback on positions C and D in two actions. When they are back at position A, the attacker and defender swap roles. The athletes rotate clockwise over the positions after each action.

The camera perspective shown in Fig. 6.28 enables the athletes to visualize the action without mental rotation effort. From this perspective, the position of the arms can be recognized and corrected very well. However, if other aspects are to be addressed in this action, such as distance to the opponent, the camera perspective must be changed so that this distance is visible (e.g., camera in position D to film position A).

Athletic Training in Beach Handball

The athletic demands that beach handball places on the athletes are variable, similar to another handball discipline, indoor handball. Strength, skills, speed, and endurance are required to create basic agility that makes the game feasible. Because agility in the area of speed is not determined only by motor skills, but also by cognitive components, deficits in the areas of strength and speed can often be compensated without any problems, especially in the beginner domain.

The lack of direct body contact, compared to indoor handball, reduces the strength requirements of the athletes to mainly moving their own body and handling the ball. Especially in the lower extremities, strength skills are required that allow changes of direction and jumps on the soft, variable, and yielding sand. This surface, however, also challenges the upper body in particular, as the entire body, permanently and more strongly than on an indoor floor, must be kept stable. Landing on the sand, which is not always done on the legs, can also make special demands on the stability of one's own body.

As the sand as a yielding, soft surface takes up a lot of applied energy, jumping or sprinting movements can often be characterized as a maximum intensive application of force. This yielding surface must be considered, especially with regard to the training of fast-acting movements.

In beach handball, strength training that is only designed to increase mass is useful to a very limited extent as increased body mass can always be at the expense of braking and acceleration abilities (jumping, change of direction). Instead, strength training should focus on maximum and rapid strength processes. This need is also confirmed by studies on the body constitution of beach handball players at the highest performance level: beach handball players have the same body size as indoor handball players, but they are on average 5% to 10% lighter.

The athletes' endurance is challenged intermittently. Short, but mostly high-intensity movement phases (sprints, jumps, change of direction) are followed to the same extent by low-intensity phases of rest (walking, standing, kneeling). This sequence corresponds, more or less, to the requirements of indoor handball. Thus, aerobic as well as anaerobic energy supply processes are required to resist the onset of fatigue. These phases in alternating intensities should be considered when planning endurance training. High-volume endurance training at low intensities always contributes to the improvement of basic endurance skills, but interval training is closer to the training requirements for beach handball athletes.

Methodical and content-related suggestions are made in this section in the context of user-focused athletic training, which makes beach handball-specific athletic training possible economically.

Fig. 6.29 Stabilization exercise in beach handball

Mobility and Stability Through Mobilization and Activation

The content described in Chap. 3 for the structure and design of a warm-up emphasizes and trains basic mobility and stability components. These abilities can be easily extended by a variety of support exercises, which are performed alone or with a partner (see Fig. 6.29). Classic gymnastic exercises can be used effectively here. However, forms of exercise that originate from Yoga or Pilates movement can also be efficient. Calisthenics can also be integrated into mobilizing and stabilizing training programs. Dynamic stretching methods should be preferred to static ones; although the latter do not have a negative training effect, these are less suited to the requirements of beach handball. To effectively implement stabilization and flexibility training, the following aspects should be considered:

- Any form of exercise or movement must be performed with full concentration on the affected muscles and the involved joints.
- The full range of a joint movement should always be used without exceeding pain thresholds.
- Routines are important, and space should be made for individually favoured forms of exercise or movement.
- Regardless, forms of exercise and movement should be varied and adapted again and again.
- Breathing should be kept calm and constant even in intensive holding exercises.

Linear Maximum Sprint

During a sprint, the body must be accelerated to maximum speed in the shortest possible time, and this speed must be maintained over relatively short time intervals or distances. The faster an athlete runs, the higher are the forces that have to be compensated by the muscles of his (entire) body. This force is therefore also trained. If you go into a simple linear sprint training to train not only the legs, but also the rest of the body, some aspects should be considered:

- The higher the speed, the higher the force effect on the whole body. The sprint must be performed at maximum possible speed (100%).
- For every 10 m sprinted at maximum speed, there should be 1 min of rest.
- The number of repetitions should be maintained so that fatigue does not lead to slower paces.
- Sprints with the ball should be avoided; maximum speeds are difficult to generate when holding a ball.
- A sprinted distance of 8 to 10 m per repetition is sufficient.
- Perform braking actively, and thus make it effective as strength training.

The beach handball court with its 27-m length offers optimal possibilities for linear sprint training. Starting the sprint at a goal line, an athlete needs about 10 m to accelerate to his/her maximum speed. He/she then holds this speed over the field and actively brakes when the other goal area is reached.

So that linear sprint training is also motivating and leads to 100% of the sprint speed, it is recommended that it always be carried out as a competition.

Double Legged Rotation Jumps

The two-legged jump with rotation is an athletic pre-exercise for the spin shot. The amount of force used to initiate the rotation and also the amount of force used in stopping the rotation after landing is extremely high for the entire body, and thus trains relevant muscles efficiently with repetition. To make the effect of jumps with rotation as effective as strength training, the following basic aspects should be considered:

– The higher the jump and the faster the rotation, the stronger the effect on the body will be, not only activation of the acceleration but also of the landing and braking forces.
– All jumps must be performed under maximum control (tension in the body).
– The number of repetitions should be maintained so that fatigue does not lead to a loss of control.
– Landing and braking must be performed in an active and controlled manner.
– The number of rotations should always be balanced in both directions. If you do 10 jumps with rotation to the right, you must also do 10 jumps with rotation to the left.
– The arms can be used actively as a swing element or they can be used passively (stable). Passively holding the arms in a stable position makes the rotation jump much more difficult but also increases the force required for acceleration.

Maximum Jumps in Different Vectors

Jumping off in the sand, whether done with one leg or both, requires enormous amounts of force if it is done to the maximum. Landing after the jump on the uneven sand also requires a great deal of force to bring the body back into balance. Maximum jumps should be executed either with maximum height or with maximum distance.

The combination of maximum height and maximum distance is also effective, of course. However, jumps should be executed in all possible vectors (forwards, backwards, sideways, diagonally), whereby it must be considered that jumping backwards is a great challenge for beginners in terms of coordination and can, therefore, only be implemented with maximum strength to a limited extent. To make jumping training effective not only for improving jumping strength but also as strength training for the entire body, the following aspects must be taken into account:

- Jump height and/or distance should always be maximum.
- Landing should be fully focused and deliberate.
- The number of repetitions should be maintained so that fatigue does not cause loss of control.
- Jump direction (vectors) should be balanced: jumps to the right must be balanced with jumps to the left.
- The jump directions (vectors) should be variable, but the jumps must be executed maximally.
- The frequency of one-legged jumps should be balanced (five jumps left + five jumps right).
- The use of tubes or terra bands as resistance can increase the effect on upper body effort.

Basic athletic training in beach handball. Vid 07 Standbild. (▶ https://doi.org/10.1007/000-6c6)

High-Intensity Interval Training

In high-intensity interval training to promote endurance, the cardiovascular system should be challenged with alternating loads and pauses. The high-intensity phases are most easily achieved through running elements, but other forms of movement can be used. When running, linear running sequences should not always be used; short distances, changes of direction, running backwards, and jumping, in all directions, should be used. Game forms (tag games, transition games with ball) can also be used, but it must be guaranteed that the athletes are in motion with maximum intensity. For high-intensity interval training to be effective, the following aspects should be considered:

- In intensive phases, it is necessary to work at the highest intensity (100%).
- The duration of the intensive phases should be between 10 and 30 s.
- The duration of the breaks should correspond to the duration of the load phases, but this can also be varied.
- The total duration of the load should be increased slowly and adapted to the corresponding stage of development. The total duration of the load (time of work on 100%) of 15 min does not need to be exceeded.
- It must always be ensured that the athletes are safe and healthy throughout the intensive phases. Tag games require a high level of attention and should, therefore, take place at the beginning of such training. Simple running forms can still be implemented well even when fatigued.

Coaching in Competition

Many of the coaching cues described so far in the book can also be applied to competitive coaching. In particular, information on giving feedback and making corrections or on attracting attention is also relevant in competition. Also, coaching tips and recommendations should be given here that primarily relate to the competition. Because competitions are always held in tournament forms, this competition structure must be considered in coaching. Depending on the level of performance, tournaments can last between two and four days, and two to four matches are organized per day. However, day tournaments can also be found in the competition calendar.

Coaching Tasks in and Around the Competition

Team Meetings
A distinction is made here between pre-game briefings and game debriefings. In the pre-game briefing, the circumstances of the game must be set out, and the game tasks and objectives should be made clear. Part of the pre-game briefing is also the definition of game positions and functions (starting formation). The tactical alignment can, if feasible, also be video based.

In the game debriefing, players should not be overloaded with information. However, from a psychological perspective, a brief discussion of elements such as praise, consolation, correction, and, if relevant, constructive criticism should take place. When debriefing, it is important to always focus on the next game. It is quite possible that the next game will have to be played as soon as two hours later.

Fig. 6.30 The team time-out as an effective tool to influence the game play (Photo: EHF)

Game Control

In game control, it is the coach's task to observe the course of the game analytically, to give advice to one's own team, or to influence the game through substitution or tactical adaptions.

In addition, team time-outs (1 per set) can be used to make necessary changes (see Fig. 6.30). During this time, spoken instruction should be reduced to only the essentials.

In the break between sets, there is also the opportunity to positively affect the game of your team. Five minutes are available, but only the essentials should be focused on here as well. Although it is critical to address the team's potential, their strengths must be emphasized, and how these should be best used against the opponent in the second set has to be discussed.

In the event of a shoot-out situation, the coach not only has to name the five players but must also determine the roles for these players, which is key to the team's performance. During the shoot-out, after each situation which action is most likely to succeed next (e.g., 1-point versus 2-point attempt, saving goalkeeper versus blocking defender) must be analysed. These actions must be clarified directly with the team. The score and the number of shooters must always be carefully observed.

Coaches' View

In the decision-making process of every sports coach, visual perception of the game situation is a crucial prerequisite for controlling actions. The cognitive factors—perception, attention, anticipation, memory, and decision—form the basis for this.

In many game situations, there is not enough time to perceive and process all the visual stimuli occurring on the playing field at the same time and to carefully weigh

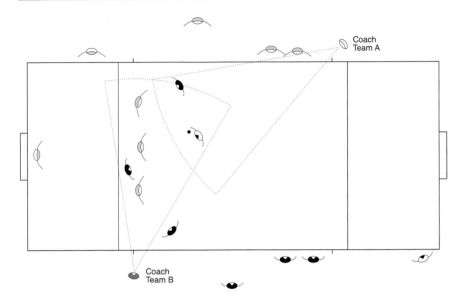

Fig. 6.31 The influence of different viewing positions on the perception of depth and breadth in the coaching role

alternative courses of action. If all the visual stimuli of a game situation were perceived, this would very quickly lead to an overload, causing restriction of the coach's ability to make decisions. To prevent this, a coach directs his/her attention to certain sub-areas to reduce the amount of information. This diversion of attention is a sensible and natural process, but it can be a disadvantage for a coach if the wrong parts of the game are the focus.

Without a doubt, in beach handball it is the coach's task to extract relevant information and, thus, specific sections in his field of vision from complex game situations as quickly as possible. The goal must, therefore, be an effective visual search strategy, with which the point is not to perceive as much as possible, but to recognize decisive, game-guiding, and action-relevant signals. Here, the perspective (see Fig. 6.31) from the side-lines represents an additional challenge in contrast to a bird's-eye view. The players can concentrate their perception on other players and action on the field, but the coach has a greater challenge with his/her concentration also on the substitution area, which can have a tremendous impact on how the game is perceived.

In addition, other factors such as noise, delegates' table, referees, or spectators can make it difficult to perceive game-related actions. The coach must, therefore, be an effective information manager in terms of his/her ability to act and make decisions. Conscious guidance and control of his/her perception—the coach's view—is necessary during a game. The coach must clearly define his/her own areas of interest to get all the information necessary for optimal action and at the same time to exclude unnecessary information.

The areas of interest and the focus of the coach's attention and perception should optimally be based on the task at hand. With regard to attacking and defending play, direct play with the ball (based on the players in the vicinity of the ball) and against the ball seems to be the most relevant (see also Fig. 6.31), as this is where the most directly measurable effects on game performance take place (goal versus no goal).

Actions away from the ball, such as running into spaces in attack or closing gaps in the defence, should also be focused on, as these can significantly influence the success of actions in the game. However, the further away these actions take place from what is happening with the ball, the more difficult simultaneous perception becomes. The coach must, therefore, decide which "area" is in his/her interest, that is, how the coach directs his/her attention. The focus of perception in defence and attack can be on one's players as well as the opposing players.

If the coach focuses on the opposing defence, weaknesses of the opponent in the tactical (e.g., certain behaviour in space) or technical (e.g., lack of footwork) areas will be noticed more quickly and the tactics of the coach's own team can be adjusted accordingly. However, it can be assumed that focusing on the opposing players can lead to distraction from one's own players. On the other hand, excessive focus on one's own players and their potential can lead to ignoring the analysis of the defensive strategies of the opposing team. Therefore, a balance should be maintained.

A conscious discussion during a game should, therefore, be part of the coaching match plan. The general strategy seems to be decisive here, that is, whether the coaching is more success oriented or development oriented. In terms of success orientation, it is advisable to direct one's perception in such a way that the weaknesses of the opponent are revealed. In the sense of a development orientation, the perception should be directed to one's team to reveal the technical-tactical potential promptly and precisely and to develop this immediately in the game or training operation.

The following recommendations for action are summarized for the coach's view

- Position yourself so that you can see as much of the game-relevant action as possible. Also consider changing the game phases (attack, defence, transition, goalkeeping).
- Remember that your position influences the perception of depth and breadth. If you are also at the height of the game plot, your depth perception is better; if you are as orthogonal to it as possible, your width perception is better (Fig. 6.31).
- Try to keep the influence of external disturbances low. Keep your perception on the line; refrain from focusing on the stands, referees, or delegates, and the substitutes.

(continued)

- Direct your focus only on actions relevant to the game. Observe what you think is important.
- Orient yourself to your coaching match plan (opponent orientation versus development orientation of your own team).
- Train your perception, especially during training games.
- In addition to focusing on direct actions at the ball location, you can also try to keep an eye on actions away from the ball, which significantly influence the success of actions that are effective in the game.

Game Analysis

With regard to a systematic game analysis in beach handball, the game idea and the rules relating to space, time, and situations should be seen as the basis. As beach handball is characterized by a high density of events in the area of goal closing actions (sometimes more than two goal shots per minute), the match analysis must be based on the probability of success.

Thus, the game analysis must focus on which actions, in which space, in which situation, and at what point in time occur, what points are scored on one hand, and what attacks are defended, or balls captured, on the other.

Using the example of a spin shot (action), it would be necessary to record for the game analysis whether the shot was successful (0, 1, or 2 points), where the shot took place (space; e.g., outside or central), when the shot took place (time), and at what score (situation). It should also be recorded who performed this spin shot and whether, for example, there was a block in the defence.

If one considers a large number of such situations, the game analysis can make a statement about how effective (points scored) a spin shot is in different spaces, at certain times, or in certain situations. Such a game analysis should be applied to all game phases (attack, defence, transition).

A separate analysis is recommended for the goalkeeping game, which is examined again in two different situations. In the first part, game actions where there is cooperation with one's team should be analysed (e.g., block agreements, game-opening). In the second part, an individualized analysis should be made for all game actions in which the goalkeeper acts alone against the shooter (e.g., free throws, 6 m, coast-to-coast attempts). It is important to have a clear definition of the term save. In addition to saved balls (the goalkeeper touches the ball), there are also a large number of balls in the game that go next to or over the goal. The influence of a goalkeeper on such balls is difficult to measure objectively. Therefore, it is recommended to use a gross (all balls were thrown in the direction of the goal) and net (all balls which

(continued)

the goalkeeper has touched) statistic with regard to the saves. By weighing the gross and net saves, performance of an athlete in the goalkeeper position can be measured successfully.

Because the shoot-out is a special situation, albeit with the same relevance as playing in the sets, this should be taken into account in the game analysis.

In combination with the subjective impression of the coach, relevant information for (a) training content and (b) action in the competition can be derived from this game analysis. In the game analysis, the primary focus needs to be identified and considered. If it is geared towards performing competition diagnostics to evaluate the performance level of your team (a), the focus is primarily on the athletes of your team. Training content and methods can then be derived from the data obtained to improve the performance of your athletes. If the analysis is for competition diagnostics (b), the opposing athletes primarily come into focus. The analysis should show where the strengths, and especially the weaknesses, of the opponents lie.

Especially with the opponent-focused game analysis, the structure of the tournament forms must be considered and observed. Because beach handball tournaments are usually played over 2 to 4 days with two to four games per day, this analysis requires a time-efficient and economical approach. The methods are mainly determined by the available data. As there is hardly any automated data collection in beach handball (mostly only analogous to the score and the course of the game at the delegate's table), data must be collected through subjective observation during the games or post hoc with video analyses. It should be noted that during a tournament there is only a limited time for post hoc video analysis; this method is more relevant for game analysis to derive training content. The live analysis is significantly more relevant during a tournament (see Fig. 6.32).

Fig. 6.32 Using software solutions to simplify the game analysis

Simple paper-and-pencil procedures can be used as a methodological resource for this. However, a large number of cost-effective technology solutions enable live analysis with direct data input. These systems are mostly used in other sports, including indoor handball, but can also be used in beach handball. Such systems often not only allow digital input of the data, but also, combined with a video stream, live tagging of game scenes, which can then be used in the subsequent analysis.

In conclusion, however, it must be stated that in game analysis, user-friendliness and the focus on benefits are paramount. The most detailed game analysis has no added value if the data obtained cannot be used for competition or training. Each coach must begin by clearly defining the game actions for which he/she needs a supporting evaluation through a game analysis to achieve individual goals. Because these are very different, the only relevant concern is to develop a time-efficient method of game analysis that is suitable for one's own coaching.

Further Readings

Hughes M, Franks I (2015) Essentials of performance analysis in sport. Routledge, Abingdon
McGarry T, O'Donoghue P, Sampaio J (2013) Routledge handbook of sports performance analysis. Routledge, Abingdon

Basics in Beach Handball Refereeing, Organization, and Recommendations of Literature

7

Contents

The Beach Handball Officials

> The following chapter provides insight into the role of referees and officials in beach handball. In addition to the relevance of referees for the conduct of a match, aspects of their training are presented. Further, basic behaviours for managing a match are suggested, and also the most relevant referee hand signals are illustrated.

The following chapter provides insight into the role of referees and officials in beach handball. In addition to the relevance of referees for the conduct of a match, aspects of their training are presented. Further, basic behaviours for managing a

Fig. 7.1 Referees, more than a relevant part of the game (Photo: EHF)

Fig. 7.2 Beach handball officials at the Beach Handball EURO 2021 (Photo: EHF)

match are suggested and also the most relevant referee hand signals are illustrated
(see Fig. 7.1).

Referees, or officials, are a fundamental part of conducting (competitive) sports
competitions in beach handball (see Fig. 7.2). They are installed to ensure that the
competition takes place following the rules, in a fair and healthy manner, and should

allow the better man to win. However, referees in particular are usually only given greater attention by the public when they make mistakes that may even have a decisive influence on the final result of a competition. Even if they perform excellently throughout the entire match but make an unfortunate decision in the last action of the game, it is precisely this decision that serves as the yardstick for the overall impression for most of those involved. However, the fact that referees can also make a very important contribution or even the prerequisite for the success of an exciting and dynamic game is often neglected here. With consistent rule interpretation, skilful game management, open and positive charisma, and consistent and transparent communication, referees contribute greatly to successful and joyful competitions.

In addition to the motivation to become involved as a referee for beach handball, good and comprehensive training is above all relevant for the management of competitions. Internationally, special courses for beach handball officials were offered early on. For example, the EHF organized the first "Beach Handball Referee & Delegate's Course" in 1999 with great interest and success, and further courses have followed at regular intervals since then. The IHF has also offered courses for officials since the 2004 World Championships. At the national and regional level, players or coaches were more likely to be used to officiate matches in the beginning; this seemed more sensible in the early years than retraining indoor handball referees. Players and coaches who themselves had experience with beach handball certainly developed a very good "feeling" for the game. It was only later that national and regional associations established referee courses and a structured refereeing system. In addition to the development of the rules and regulations, a development of the sport of beach handball can also be observed in this area.

Beach handball referees must be very familiar with the standard set of rules to avoid ambiguities and possible discrepancies. On an international level, regular online training courses and tests are held for this purpose. In addition, the idea of spectacular and fast play should always be focused for all participants; that is, spectacular actions such as inflights and spin shots should be rewarded. Interruptions of the fast game by unnecessary whistling are to be avoided; penalties can also be given after completed actions.

In addition, it is the referee's job to immediately stop rough fouls in particular. It must be made clear to the teams from the start of a beach handball game that fouls are undesirable and will be punished directly, and that the philosophy of the game must be respected at all times. For marketing reasons, beach handball referees should also always be a bit of an entertainer on the field. Two-point scores can also be displayed spectacularly and the audience may be carried away as a result.

The referees are assisted by two other officials on the court, namely, the timekeeper and the secretary. In addition to the notation of the score, the technical officials' table also has the task of monitoring the players' suspensions and indicating them to the referees. Furthermore, the technical officials' table also monitors the transition area. At international events, technical delegates are also deployed. The tasks of a technical delegate are, among others, to ensure the smooth flow of a match, to ensure compliance with the regulations, and to be the contact person for timekeeper/secretary, referees, and teams. Last but not least, the technical

Fig. 7.3 Special referee hand signals in beach handball

delegate is to ensure the safety of players, referees, and spectators together with the tournament organizer.

The scores of points and penalties are indicated by the referees in beach handball with different gestures and signs to avoid confusion. To facilitate the work of the referees and the secretaries, the two-point indication, for example, must be different from the one-point indication. The IHF rulebook states: "If 1 or 2 points are credited when a goal is scored then the court referee must indicate this by displaying 1 or 2 fingers. When 2 points are awarded, the goal referee does a full vertical arm swing additionally" (IHF 2021, p. 36). Furthermore, the IHF rulebook lists and illustrates all hand signals in beach handball (IHF 2021, pp. 36–44); the main differences from indoor handball are the following three hand signals (see Fig. 7.3).

In summary, the following basic aspects can be noted for successful game management in the role of the referee.

- The referee must have adequate knowledge of the rules and be able to apply them in an adapted manner if necessary.
- The referee should always position himself/herself so that he/she has an optimal view of the game. When two referees are in charge of a match, a distinction is made between field and goal referees (see Fig. 7.4).
- If the game is in progress, the whistle should be blown loudly (!) in case of a rule violation.
- Immediately after the whistle, the direction of play in which the game continues should be displayed. In the beginner area, this should be displayed until the players continue the game on their own. In general, if necessary, the whistle can be repeated with the appropriate IHF hand signal.
- The referee should act at all times courageously, consistently, and with a correspondingly clear body language.

(continued)

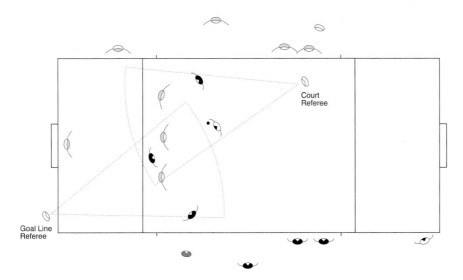

Fig. 7.4 Positioning of the referees for an optimal view of the game

- The referee must decide impartially. This impartiality can be purposefully adapted in training and competition, especially with children, for pedagogical reasons.
- Beginners, children, and young people should also have rules violations explained to them during the competition. However, this should only be done to an extent that does not disturb the flow of the game and the playing experience. The referee thus also contributes to the development of the playing ability of beginners.
- Good and open communication with players and team managers continues to be helpful. In the event of ambiguities, brief explanations are extremely effective for learning.

A good referee is not a rules policeman but takes an active, formative role in the game. His or her way of refereeing and managing the game is elementary to transport the philosophy of beach handball and to make it realizable. "Refereeing" in beach handball is therefore not a purely mathematical-scientific task but rather a complex compositional art form. Interaction with the competition, the athletes, and all others involved is characterized in beach handball with great respect for each other and a shared love of the game. When this attitude is shared by referees, athletes, coaches, and spectators, it increases the value of the referee role in beach handball.

Recommendations for Setting Up Beach Handball Courts

The construction of beach handball facilities is described next, referring to temporary installations on the beach and in other environments as well as to the construction of permanent installations. In addition to information on dimensions and materials, tips for implementing the construction are provided.

Construction of a (Temporary) Beach Handball Court (for Example, on the Beach)

Before you set up a beach handball court, you have to make a few considerations. The IHF rules state: "The playing surface must be composed of levelled sand, as flat and uniform as possible, free of rocks, shells and anything else, which can represent risks of cuts or injuries to the players. The sand must be of at least 40 cm deep and composed of fine loosely compacted grains. The court should run lengthwise north–south. The characteristics of the playing court must not be altered during the game in such a way that one team gains an advantage. There should be a safety zone with a width of 3 m surrounding the playing court." (IHF 2021).

There are beach handball goals and beach handball line systems from various manufacturers that are easy to anchor in the sand; however, for safety and stability reasons, the anchors of the line systems and the goals should be buried at least 40 cm deep. Once you have found a suitable area on the beach, you must pay particular attention to the north–south orientation of the playing field (because of sunshine) and the level of the ground. Ideally, (mobile) safety nets are attached behind the goals. You should clear the place (preferably with a rake) of coarse rock and shards or shells, and then the field is playable (see Fig. 7.5).

Setting Up a Temporary Beach Handball Court (for Example, in the City)

When a temporary beach handball court is built up (for example, on the market square of a city), it is usually about an event to attract spectators to cities or public places. A safety distance of 3.0 m to the playing field on all sides should therefore be satisfied with all set-ups. In addition to the points mentioned in the following, a solid and level surface (e.g., asphalt), a stable border (e.g., a wooden plank tub), and the right choice of quartz sand must be observed. One should calculate with a sand height of at least 50 cm, and therefore at least 250 tons of sand will be needed.

Fig. 7.5 Temporary beach handball courts at the Beach Handball EURO 2021 (Photo: EHF)

Construction of a Permanent Beach Handball Facility (for Example, on a Sports Field)

First of all, you should plan the plant construction in terms of time, personnel, and space. The time frame should be estimated at 2 to 3 months, depending on the available workforce. With a total of about 800 hours of work, this planning is realistic. Once one has found the right site and the necessary helpers, one should draw up a detailed construction plan (with a top view and cross section) of the beach facility.

First, an excavation pit with the following dimensions must be dug:

Depth: at least 0.70 m.
Length: at least 33.00 m.
Width: at least 18.00 m.

The excavated soil can be used to fill a wall (spectator stand) on one long side of the playing field. The excavated construction pit is then bordered with a wooden plank tub or plastic pipes; stone slabs are not recommended because of the increased risk of injury (see Fig. 7.6).

The excavation pit is then filled with a layer of gravel 0.30 m deep. It is advisable to store drainage pipes in the gravel layer on the slope and to connect them to any existing drainage system on the sports field (see Fig. 7.7). Two goal sleeves embedded in concrete are now dug into the two front sides. Special beach handball

Fig. 7.6 Excavation of the construction pit (Photo: Alex Gehrer)

Fig. 7.7 Gravel layer and drainage pipes (Photo: Alex Gehrer)

Fig. 7.8 Safety fences on the beach handball court (Photo: Alex Gehrer)

goals are available from various manufacturers. It also makes sense to attach sleeves for volleyball posts in this step.

Now, a water-permeable fleece is placed to hold back the sand. When placing the fleece, make sure that no holes are torn in the fleece with a shovel or spade: Then, 0.40 m of quartz sand (170–200 t) is poured onto the fleece. Pay attention to the even distribution of the sand; it is usually in the middle of the square that the tub descends most. In the case of quartz sand, sand washed several times, with a grain size of 0.5 mm to 1.0 mm, has proven to be optimal (this is also the recommendation of the IHF).

It is advisable to erect a safety fence 3 to 5 m high behind each of the goals (see Fig. 7.8). This fence has two functions. The annoying fetching of the ball after missed throws is no longer necessary, so the fast counter-attack game is maintained. In addition, such a safety fence is the ideal place to attach sponsors' gangs or floodlights at midnight tournaments.

Recommendations for Organizing a Tournament

The organization of a beach handball tournament is a very nice and exciting affair, but it also requires much effort. Good and structured planning in terms of objectives, time, processes, finances, structure, and implementation makes this effort much easier. The following chapter, therefore, provides information and help for the organization of a tournament.

Overall Aim

When organizing your beach handball tournament, there are a few basic things to consider. Before starting the concrete planning, you have to think about the target group (youth tournament or adult tournament, number of participating teams, supporting program, etc.). The number of courts required and the general conditions then depend on this. In addition, you have to consider whether the tournament is to be organized as a pure fun tournament or as part of a national (e.g., ARENA Beach Tour in Spain or GERMAN BEACH OPEN in Germany) and/or an international (e.g., EUROPEAN BEACH TOUR in Europe) tournament series. With these tournament series, there are clear minimum criteria catalogues that a tournament must contain in any case; in addition, you can acquire points for additional services for the tournament ranking. For example, there are points for safety nets behind the goals, live streams, and electronic scoreboards.

Creation of a Beach Handball Atmosphere

Regardless of the criteria catalogues of various tournament series, music and atmosphere are important if you want to develop your tournament into an event. The corresponding framework conditions (catering, beach bar, family activities, competitions, sponsorship events, etc.) round off the event (see Figs. 7.9 and 7.10).

Promotion

Once you have decided on a type of tournament (adults/youth, number of participants, part of a tournament series), the next step is detailed planning. The announcement of the tournament runs for logical reasons via a homepage on which participating teams can register and which is then linked to the tournament series if necessary.

Fig. 7.9 Beach handball atmosphere at the Junior European Championships 2021 in Varna, Bulgaria (Photo: EHF)

Fig. 7.10 Final match of the men's tournament at the Beach Handball EURO 2021 (Photo: EHF)

Structure and Timing

In addition to the match schedule, the number of participating teams also determines the need for playing courts. In beach handball, 16 teams have proven to be optimal. In four groups of four, the two group leaders advance and play crosswise (always first against second) quarter-finals. The winners go to the semi-finals; the losers also play for the places 5–8. At the end of the tournament, there is always a final. This knockout system also corresponds to the basic idea of the game beach handball, according to which there is always a winner after a game. All teams are guaranteed a minimum of 3 matches (in the group stage) and a maximum of 6 matches (up to the final). The net time required for a 16-team tournament with a generously calculated time interval of 35 min per match is a total of 21 hours (on one playing field) with 36 matches (24 matches in the group phase, 4 quarter-finals, 4 matches for places 5–8, 2 semi-finals, 1 match for third place, and 1 final).

Courts and Costs

Thus, for example, for a 2-day tournament with two times 16 teams (male and female), at least two courts are required (see Fig. 7.11). If you are planning additional activities (youth games, mini-beach handball, etc.), a third court can be used. The following costs should be taken into account in your calculation for a tournament with two courts (see Table 7.1):

In addition, there are costs for staff (referees, technical officials, tournament organization, helpers, DJ/moderator). On the other hand, there are numerous possible sources of income (stalls, sponsors, beach bar, food and drink sales, merchandising, possibly overnight stays).

Fig. 7.11 Beach handball goals and line system (Photo: Alex Gehrer)

Table 7.1 Hardware costs for two beach handball courts

Cost calculation for two beach handball courts	
4 Beach handball goals (with goal nets)	approx. € 3000 to € 4000
2 line systems	approx. € 500 to € 1000
20 beach handballs	approx. € 500 to € 1000
4 safety nets behind the goals	approx. € 2000 to € 3000
2 tents (tournament office, DJ/moderator) for rent	approx. € 2000 to € 3000
In total	approx. € 8000 to € 12,000

The Beach Handball Literature

In the following chapter, recommendations are given for further literature from different language and cultural areas. The main focus is on literature that covers the beginners' area, the structures, and the organization in beach handball. Many of these literature references can also be seen as a source of ideas for this book. The presented works should cover different language and cultural areas, depending on the availability of the sources (see Fig. 7.12). No qualitative evaluation of the works is made here, and no other works are to be neglected. Rather, the sources available at the time of the publication of this book have been prepared here.

The Fédération Française de Handball has published an interactive practice guide in French. In addition to a short insight into the history and philosophy of beach handball, the structures of French beach handball up to international competitions are presented. Furthermore, recommendations for the organization and construction of beach handball facilities are given. However, the largest part of this practical guide relates to the training and development of beach handball skills and abilities. What makes this guide particularly attractive is its interactivity; specific content is linked to videos on a platform, making the content also vivid in moving images.

Fédération Française de Handball (2021). *Beach Handball. Guide de la pratique.* Creteil: FFHandball.

Fig. 7.12 The internationality of beach handball is also represented in the literature (Photo: EHF)

The Federação Paulista de Handebol from Brazil has published a work in Portuguese for the promotion and development of beach handball in the age range 5 to 10 years. The focus of this work is on organizational, methodological, and didactic advice for beach handball in the children's area. Especially, adaptations of the game to a mini-beach handball game are described, and teaching-learning hints for teachers or coaches are given. The work is also translated into Spanish.

Saraiva, J. A., Francavilla, L. B., Cardozo Júnior, J. N., Vieira de Camargo, B. J., dos Santos, J. G. (2020). *Mini Beach Handball*. São Paulo: Federação Paulista de Handebol.

The *Handball On Hand* e-book is available in English, Spanish, Portuguese, and Polish. It lists and explains basic aspects of the philosophy of the game and the basic rules. Further, the specifics of the game on a tactical level are discussed. The basic technical elements of individual defensive and offensive play are presented with a series of pictures, tips, and training recommendations.

Magliano, M. (2019). *Beach Handball. On Hands*. Self-published.

The Federación Madrileña de Balonmano has published a paper in Spanish on the methodological principles in the training of technical-tactical elements. Besides a short historical introduction, different works are taken up to justify the methodical approach. Based on this, methodological recommendations are presented on one hand and content-related suggestions for training on the other. For this purpose, game and exercise forms for different technical-tactical elements of beach handball are described in detail.

Zapardiel, J. C. (2018). *Propuesta de principios metodológicos para el entrenamiento técnico-táctico en balonmano playa*. Madrid: Federación Madrileña de Balonmano.

The Dansk Håndbold Forbund has published three handouts in Danish that present game forms, practice forms, and alternative movement games on the sand. These papers focus on technical-tactical elements of beach handball, but also describe general activities on the sand. In addition to detailed descriptions of the structure and implementation of the exercise and game forms, methodological-didactic tips on observation focal points and variation possibilities are shown.

Dansk Håndbold Forbund. (2021). *Beach handball træningsmaterialer*. Brøndby: DHF.

The German Handball Federation has published the *Beach Handball Training Concept* with a web-app, a multimedia work in German. Based online, technical-tactical content is presented for the development of playing ability from the child to the senior level. This content is further supported with methodical tips and basics for playing and competing in beach handball. In addition, athletic components and the personality of the athletes are presented in a targeted manner.

Deutscher Handballbund. (2021). *DHB-Rahmentrainingskonzeption Beach Handball.* Dortmund: DHB und Münster: Phillipka-Sportverlag.

The Slovenian book by Kavčič and Peterlin gives insight into the general and the regional, Slovenian history of beach handball. Further, detailed information on the structure and organization of the game is given. In addition to explanations of technical and tactical elements of the game and their training, this book also accords special attention to referees and officials. Game management by referees is thereby prepared in terms of content and graphics with the representation of the most important hand signals.

Kavčič, M., Peterlin, J. (2018). *Priročnik za trenerje, športne pedagoge, igralce insodnike.* Ljubljana: Rokometna zveza Slovenja.

The handbook *Beach Handball from A to Z* in the English language has a focus on the organizational and structural aspects of beach handball. After a short insight into the history and philosophy of beach handball, comprehensive information on event organization is given. In addition, medial and technological preparation, as well as marketing, are explained intensively. Further aspects of beach handball-specific event management, from ceremony regulations to event services such as accommodation, catering, or medical care are addressed.

Bebetsos, G. (2012). *Beach Handball from A to Z. The IHF Beach Handball handbook.* Basel: International Handball Federation.

The work *BeacHandball* is the history of the emergence of beach handball in Italian and English. Here are presented in detail basic thoughts on the development of the discipline. From the preliminary considerations for the development of the discipline, over motivational aspects up to the causes of the rulebook development are reported in this book. The first official competitions and events in the early 1990s are covered in detail, as is the implementation of the first official set of rules for the discipline of beach handball. Cardinale and Montagni already draw the first exercise-science conclusions about the effect of bounce training in the sand from test series with the Italian handball military team.

Cardinale, M., Montagni, S. (1996). *BeacHandball.* Rom: Federazione Italiana Giuoco Handball.

Further Reading

Bebetsos G (2012) Beachandball from A to Z. The IHF Beachhandball handbook. International Handball Federation, Basel

IHF (2021) Rules of the Game. Beach Handball. International Handball Federation, Basel

Livingston L, Forbes SL, Wattie N, Cunningham I (2020) Sports officiating. Re-cruitment, development, and retention. Routledge, New York

MacMahon C, Mascarenha D, Plessner H, Pizzerra A, Oudejans RRD, Raab M (2015) Sports officials and officiating: science and practice. Routledge, Abingdon

Glossary

1-Point-Goal Each goal scored is counted as 1 point.

2-Point-Goal If a goal is scored in a spectacular manner, according to the definitions of the rules, an extra point is awarded, and the goal is scored with 2 points.

6 m Penalty If a clear scoring chance is irregularly prevented, the referees must award a 6 m penalty. A player throws this penalty in a 1-on-1 situation against the goalkeeper from a standing position, positioned in front of the 6 m line. Each goal from this action is a 2-point goal.

Block A play action of a defender who blocks a ball thrown at the goal.

Block Change Principle All players of a team standing on the field leave the field after ball loss/goal and are all replaced by substitutes.

Bodiless In the defensive play, the body of the opponent is not attacked; only the ball is attacked with hands and arms. Bodiless does not mean contactless: physical contact may occur, but only by standing in the path of an attacker. This contact must also be healthy and fair at all times.

Centre A player who is positioned in the attack in the middle of the field.

Changing Player Players who are used exclusively in attack or defence. At the end of their phase of play due to the change of possession, they substitute either in or out.

Coaching Cues Behavioural and action guidelines that should simplify the coaching of athletes under psychological-pedagogical and physiological aspects.

Coast-to-Coast Goal A goal scored by a goalkeeper from within his own goal area. This goal is always a 2-point goal.

Counting Points method Game rules in which goals are scored with a different number of points, depending on their execution.

Diver Block A play action in which a defender blocks a ball thrown at the goal by jumping into his own goal area.

Empty Net Goal A goal scored by a player when the opponent's goal is unmonitored. This goal can be a 1-point goal or a 2-point goal.

Formal Rules Rules that are laid down in the rulebook and which result in clearly defined actions or sanctions in the event of violations.

F. Fasold et al., *Beach Handball for Beginners*,
https://doi.org/10.1007/978-3-662-64566-6

Game Form A game in which not all beach handball rules are applied, and the rules are adapted for training purposes.

Goalkeeper A player who is used exclusively in the defensive position of the goalkeeper. He/she wears a different coloured shirt than his or her own team.

Goal Oriented Tasks, exercises, games, and actions that have a clear (learning) goal.

Golden Goal If the score is tied at the end of a set, play continues until the next goal is scored. The team that scores this goal wins the set.

Half-Time Break between the two sets of a match (5 min).

Inflight In an inflight action, an attacker catches the ball from a pass on the bounce and throws it at the goal before he/she lands. If this results in a goal, it is a 2-point goal.

Informal Rules Rules and norms which are not laid down in the rules and regulations and which, for the most part, are not checked by a referee. Informal rules are rather behavioural guidelines that refer to the cooperation or guidelines which may have a tactical background.

Left Defence/Centre Defence/Right Defence The positioning of the players in the defence.

Line-Player A player who is positioned on the 6 m line in the attack.

Match The term refers to a beach handball game played over two sets and, if necessary, a shoot-out.

Match Point A team gets one match point for winning a set. If the score is 1:1 after both sets, the team that wins the shoot-out gets another match point and wins 2:1.

Power Position Action of an attacker with the ball in which he/she has the ball with his or her throwing arm in a position except for which he/she has all possibilities of play in the subsequent action (all passes, all throws)

Set A match consists of two sets (each 10 min) which have the same playing time but are scored independently.

Shoot-Out The shoot-out is a deciding point in a match in which, similar to the penalty shoot-out in soccer or the penalty shoot-out in ice hockey, attackers compete against a defender. A shoot-out happens when each team has won one of the two sets.

Smooth Game State of games or game forms that run without major interruptions and can be resumed quickly in the event of interruptions. All participating athletes bring the skills to implement the requirements of the games so that the game is in flow at all times.

Specialist A player who wears the same coloured shirt as the team's goalkeeper and can substitute the goalkeeper in the offense. The specialist acts purely as an attacker; if the ball is lost, he/she substitutes for his/her goalkeeper. Each goal scored by this player is a 2-point goal.

Spin Shot In the spin-shot action, an attacker with the ball makes a 360-degree turn in the air before throwing it at the goal. If this results in a goal, it is a 2-point goal.

Substitutes Players who do not actively participate in the game but can be substituted.

Transition Game Phases of the game in which the player tries to bridge the field and attack the opponent's goal as quickly as possible after winning the ball. The same applies to the defence; here the transition game describes the game phase in which after losing the ball as quickly as possible, the defensive formation is assumed.

Wing-Player A player who is positioned in the attack on the side of the field.

Index

© The Author(s), under exclusive license to Springer-Verlag GmbH, DE, part of Springer Nature 2022
F. Fasold et al., *Beach Handball for Beginners*,
https://doi.org/10.1007/978-3-662-64566-6